Weight
Training
for
Women

Weight Training *for* Women

Thomas D. Fahey
Gayle Hutchinson
California State University, Chico

MAYFIELD PUBLISHING COMPANY
MOUNTAIN VIEW, CALIFORNIA
LONDON • TORONTO

Library of Congress Cataloging-in-Publication Data

Fahey, Thomas D. (Thomas Davin)
    Weight training for women / Thomas D. Fahey, Gayle Hutchinson.
        p.   cm.
    Includes bibliographical references.
    ISBN 1–55934–048–7
    1. Weight training for women. I. Hutchinson, Gayle. II. Title.
GV546.6.W64F34   1991
613.7′045 — dc20   91–18357
                                                  CIP

Manufactured in the United States of America
10 9 8 7 6 5 4 3 2 1

Mayfield Publishing Company
1240 Villa Street
Mountain View, California 94041

Sponsoring editor, James Bull; managing editor, Linda Toy;
production editor, Sondra Glider; manuscript editor, Alice Klein;
text and cover designer, Terri Wright; illustrator, Raychel Ciemma.
Cover photo: © David Madison 1990

The text was set in 10/12 Times Roman by TypeLink and printed
on 50# Finch Opaque by Malloy Lithographing.

Contents

6   Developing the Chest and Shoulders 55

9   Developing the Abdominal Muscles 123

10   Developing the Lower Body 134

Preface

WEIGHT TRAINING HAS BECOME EXTREMELY POPULAR WITH WOMEN THROUGHOUT THE world because it helps them acquire muscle strength and power that carries over into other activities and also provides them with an effective way of developing firm, healthy looking bodies. We have attempted to provide a basic guide to weight training that furnishes everything women need to know to get started in this enjoyable and beneficial activity. Although we present the latest scientific information, we have made an effort to minimize scientific and athletic jargon so that the material is easy to understand.

Organization

Chapter 1 identifies the benefits of weight training. Chapter 2 explores the physiology of weight training and includes information about topics important to women's health, such as amenorrhea, premenstrual syndrome, osteoporosis, and pregnancy. Chapters 3 through 5 examine the principles of weight training and discuss the integration of weight training into a fitness program, the choice of a health club, the structure of a weight training program, and equipment required for the activity. Chapters 6 through 10 describe exercises to develop the muscles of the chest and shoulders, arms, neck and back, abdomen, and lower body. Chapter 11 presents important information from sports nutritionists on diet, ergogenic aids, and weight control, separating fact from fiction in this very controversial area. Appendix I illustrates the muscular system, and Appendix II presents programs tailored specifically for a number of selected activities. The book provides complete references for people who want additional information or verification of the accuracy of the material presented in the book.

Features

Weight Training for Women includes many features that make it unique among weight training books. It contains the latest information from the medical, exercise physiology, and sports medicine literature presented in a manner that is easy to understand. We discuss health issues important to women and the relationship of these issues to weight training. Our discussions of pregnancy, amenorrhea, premenstrual syndrome, and the effects of anabolic steroids on women are not covered in any other weight training book. Every exercise is described in detail and accompanied by a figure clearly showing the major muscles it develops. Descriptions of free-weight and weight machine exercises are included. Safety is stressed throughout. Caution statements are included whenever a point is particularly important for preventing injury or avoiding an accident. The appendixes include detailed anatomical drawings and suggested programs for a variety of activities. The back cover includes a workout card so that students can track their progress during the course.

Acknowledgments

Any book is the product of more than the people who wrote it. We are indebted to the people at Mayfield Publishing, including Jim Bull, Kirstan Price, Sondra Glider, and Alice Klein for their efforts in sponsoring, editing, and producing the book. We are grateful for the many suggestions made by reviewers of the manuscript: Kathy Dieringer, Texas Woman's University; Ranna Lucas, Southern Methodist University; Helene Washington, Black Hawk College; and Debra Waters, University of New Mexico. We are particularly indebted to our colleagues Bill Colvin and David Swanson for providing an enjoyable and supportive work atmosphere. Finally, it would have been impossible to write this book without our professors, coaches, and fellow athletes, who provided us with theoretical and practical knowledge. These include George Brooks, Patty Freedson, Bob Lualhati, Frank Verducci, Larry Rarick, Harmon Brown, Franklin Henry, Art Burns, John Powell, Carl Wallen, Lachsen Akka, and Tom Carey.

Weight
Training
for
Women

1

Weight Training for Women

BE HONEST WITH YOURSELF. IF YOU HAD TO APPRAISE THE REAL REASONS YOU EXERCISE, what would they be? Would preventing heart disease and bone deterioration be at the top of the list? Unless you're much different than most people, avoiding disease is not the main reason you lift weights, go to aerobics classes, run, or swim three or four days a week. Let's face it, the reason you keep coming back for more is that you want to look and feel good.

Time is a problem. Few women have enough time to spend the whole day trying to make the Olympic team. You may work, go to school, take care of the family, and follow other interests. Fortunately, you don't have to devote too much time to a fitness program to get fantastic results. The trick is to choose the right activities and design a well-structured program. Weight training can be an important part of your exercise routine.

Today weight training is generally seen as an acceptable activity for women. Sports scientists verify that women can gain strength and develop healthy-looking bodies through weight training. And modern weight training facilities provide a pleasant, congenial atmosphere in which to concentrate safely on the body parts you wish to build.

A few hours of training a week will give you a firmer, healthier-looking body as well as increased strength, which will carry over into other activities. After only a few months of weight training, you will begin to feel stronger and more confident participating in other physical activities and sports — skiing, aerobics, tennis, racquetball, volleyball, or jogging. Now is the time for you to get started and begin reaping all the benefits that weight training can provide.

There are many ways to begin a weight training program. Your options range from setting up a home gym to taking a class to joining a health spa. It is generally best to train in

1

a health club or class because you can receive expert instruction. Also, you can usually work out on better equipment than at home.

Instruction is critical. On your own, you may waste much time and effort doing poor weight training routines and end up with little to show for it. Worse, you may develop muscle or joint problems common in women, such as knee cap pain or back pain. A competent instructor can help you avoid these pitfalls. Good health clubs have qualified instructors who can set up a program tailor-made to your needs. These instructors are much better trained than in the past. Try to join a club that hires instructors who have had formal training in **exercise physiology** and sports sciences.

If motivation is a problem and you find it difficult to stay with a program, maybe a weight training class is the place for you. A class makes it easier to start a program — and stick with it. It gives you a place and time to train and someone to teach you about the basics of weight training. A class also helps motivate you to train consistently. Because you have made a basic commitment to attend the class, you are likelier to devote the time needed to meet your goal.

What if you are the solitary type who doesn't want to join a club or take a class? You can set up a home gym that can either substitute for a program at the health club or supplement your weight training class. Weight training at home is also beneficial if you have difficulty scheduling a class, if attending a spa is inconvenient, or if you don't want to spend the money for a health club membership. There is a vast array of inexpensive, high-quality home-fitness products available that can provide many benefits of a well-equipped gymnasium. To sum it up, there is a way to fit weight training into almost anyone's program.

WEIGHT TRAINING AND YOUR TOTAL PHYSICAL FITNESS PROGRAM

Weight training alone is not enough to develop and maintain optimal health and fitness. You should participate in a well-rounded health-promotion program that includes proper nutrition, good health habits, and exercise for endurance, strength, and flexibility.

Proper nutrition will supply enough energy for a healthy life-style, help you avoid or get rid of excess body fat, and prevent diseases, such as osteoporosis (bone weakness), cancer, and heart disease. A healthy life-style also includes not smoking, handling emotional stress properly, and good personal hygiene.

Endurance exercise is necessary to prevent heart disease; strengthen the heart, lungs, and blood vessels; and improve chemical regulation within the cells. Activities such as running, **aerobics**, cycling, and skiing contribute to endurance fitness, provide an enjoyable recreational outlet, and improve other components of fitness, such as muscle strength, at the same time. Flexibility training helps maintain normal joint movement, which will prevent injury and future disability (particularly as you get older). Weight training, which develops strength, is an important part of a general program to create a healthy, successful life-style.

THE BENEFITS OF WEIGHT TRAINING

Weight training provides many benefits and is a valuable component of your fitness program. These benefits include a more attractive body, increased strength and power, improved sports performance, enhanced self-image, and a competitive outlet. With weight training, almost all women can achieve rapid gains and improve themselves. This can be said of almost no other sport or form of exercise.

Weight training will help you achieve that healthy look to which most of us aspire. You can develop firm muscles, which cannot be gotten by dieting or from other forms of exercise. And because women have low levels of male hormones (androgens), you are not likely to get large or bulky muscles. Rather, you will tend to lose weight and inches, get a more defined body, and increase your strength.

But weight training will not do it all. For a fit, defined body you must watch what you eat and expend plenty of calories in endurance exercise. (And it doesn't hurt to have genetics on your side; some people are naturally fatter or thinner than the "ideal.") A combination of weight training, endurance exercise, and proper diet will improve your fitness level and tone your body.

Increased Strength and Power

Increased strength and power is an obvious advantage in daily life, in tasks ranging from carrying groceries to lifting suitcases at the airport. Everyday activities, such as unscrewing tops off jars, rearranging furniture in your house, and carrying children, are much easier if you are stronger.

But strength and power can also positively affect your health, although most people don't appreciate the role they play. For example, blood pressure increases during high-intensity upper-body exercise, such as water skiing or shoveling snow. The stronger you are, however, the less your blood pressure will increase. Every year, many people die from the effects of high blood pressure. Increased strength might help these people.

CAUTION   ◆   High blood pressure is a leading risk factor of coronary heart disease. You should not attempt to treat this problem without medical advice.

Strength training also makes muscles, tendons, and ligaments stronger and less susceptible to injury. While this is of obvious benefit in sports, it may also protect you from injury and disability related to everyday activities. Studies show that women who are stronger than average are much less susceptible to back pain. (Back pain affects over 85 percent of the American public.)

Improved Sports Performance

Have you ever skied, hiked, or played tennis with someone with poor muscle strength? They tire more easily and are less effective in the activity. People with stronger muscles hit a tennis ball harder, climb more easily to the top of the mountain, and get over the edge of a ski better. Athletes in most sports have known for years that strength training improves performance. In **strength-speed** sports, such as track and field, weight training is a cornerstone of the conditioning program.

Weight training can also help you in endurance sports, such as distance running and swimming. A weak person has to use a greater percentage of her total strength than a strong person, which compromises endurance. In endurance sports, great emphasis has been placed on the fitness of the heart and lungs. However, success also depends upon the ability to achieve and maintain a fast running or swimming speed. This is dependent, largely, on muscle strength. The best way to build strength for these sports is weight training.

Whether you are an athlete or a woman who likes to play sports recreationally, increased strength can improve your performance. Staying in shape through sports is a lot more fun than doing boring exercise routines for the sake of health. Weight training enhances your enjoyment of sports by making you more successful and capable of handling more advanced techniques.

Enhanced Self-Image

Everyone likes to feel special and unique. There are few things that improve self-image more than having a sleek, healthy-looking body. And few activities affect the body so quickly and positively as weight training. Weight training provides benefits that everyone can see in a short time.

Women who develop attractive, fit, and healthy-looking bodies naturally feel good about themselves. Many women who take up weight training find it a good form of personal therapy and radiate self-confidence.

Competitive Outlet

Weight training can provide women with a competitive outlet. Some women use weight training to give them a competitive edge in their favorite sport. Others compete directly in weight training activities, such as body building and competitive weight lifting.

Competitive weight lifting and **body building** for women are recent phenomena. The first competitions for women in these sports were held in the early 1970s. Body building has become extremely popular all over the world.

Even women who are only casually interested in weight training can get satisfaction from the competitive aspects of the activity. When you lift weights, you are competing against yourself for ''PRs'' (personal records). You are always trying to lift a little more weight or do a few more repetitions. There is no more important competition than that which you have against yourself.

LET'S GET STARTED!

Before you can get the most from your fitness program, you have to be informed. You should know basic weight training terms and understand how weight training affects your muscles, nerves, and joints. You should know where to train and what clothes to wear. Don't worry about it! In the next few chapters, we will introduce you to the basics of weight training so you can get started.

References

Brooks, G. A., and T. D. Fahey. 1987. *Fundamentals of human performance*. New York: Macmillan.

Brown, R. D., and J. M. Harrison. 1986. "The effects of a strength training program on the strength and self-concept of two female age groups." *Res. Quart. Sport. Exerc*. 57: 315–20.

Duff, R. W., and L. K. Hong. 1984. "Self images of women bodybuilders." *Soc. Sport J*. 1: 374–80.

Fahey, T. D. 1989. *Basic weight training*. Mtn. View, Calif.: Mayfield Publishing Co.

Holloway, J., A. Beuter, and J. L. Duda. 1988. "Self efficacy and training for strength in adolescent girls." *J. Appl. Sport. Psych*. 18: 699–719.

National Strength and Conditioning Association. 1989. "Strength training for female athletes: A position paper: Part I." *Nat. Strength Conditioning Assoc. J*. 11: 43–56.

Shangold, M., and G. Mirkin. 1988. *Women and exercise: Physiology and sports medicine*. Philadelphia: F. A. Davis Co.

Trujillo, C. 1983. "The effect of weight training and running exercise intervention on the self-esteem of college women." *Int. J. Sport. Psych*. 14: 162–73.

2
Weight Training and Your Body

WEIGHT TRAINING AFFECTS MORE THAN YOUR MUSCLES. IT ALSO STRENGTHENS TENDONS and ligaments, improves coordination between the nervous and muscular systems, and affects certain conditions specific to women, such as pregnancy and menstruation. In this chapter, we present a primer of the effects of weight training on your body.

RESPONSES OF WOMEN TO WEIGHT TRAINING

Many women fear that weight training will develop large, bulky muscles. While your muscles can get larger from weight training, most women don't have to worry about excessive development. The exceptions are those women who train at extreme intensities over many years, are susceptible to rapid muscle growth, or take **anabolic steroids**. Scientific studies of women weight trainers have shown that they tend to lose body fat and increase muscle mass slowly. Almost all women can expect firmer-looking bodies and increased strength without bulging muscles.

You build strength in two ways: by increasing muscle size and by improving the way the nervous system transmits information to the muscles. In women, improved function of the nervous system is *relatively* more important for strength development than it is in men. Because women do not have the same capacity as men for increasing muscle size, the relative contribution of improved nervous system function becomes more important.

How Strong Can You Get?

Pound for pound of muscle, women have nearly the same capacity to gain strength as men. Men are generally stronger, however, because they are typically bigger and have larger muscles. However, when strength is expressed per unit of cross-sectional area of muscle tissue, men are only 1–2 percent stronger than women in the upper body and about equal to women in the lower body. Also, even though muscle fibers are larger in men, metabolic function within the cells is the same in both sexes.

Can women develop large muscles from weight training? Most studies show that women don't get big muscles, but empirical evidence suggests that they can. Just look at the top women body builders. Some of them have taken anabolic steroids, but many muscular women have not taken these drugs. However, it is difficult for women to gain much muscle without training intensely over many years.

Women have trouble developing upper body strength because most of their muscle mass is in the lower body. Men have a lot of muscle and therefore more strength in their upper bodies than do women. Two factors that explain these disparities between the sexes are androgen levels and speed of nervous control of muscle.

Androgens promote the growth of muscle tissue. Androgen levels in males are about six to ten times higher than in women, so men tend to have larger muscles. Also, the male nervous system can activate muscles faster, so men tend to have more **power** (power is the ability to exert force rapidly).

Scientists still have a lot to learn before they can state precisely why men are stronger than women. But the bottom line is that women can gain much strength from weight training.

MUSCLE STRUCTURE AND STRENGTH

Muscles serve to move the skeleton. Muscles are attached to bones by tendons. When a muscle contracts, it shortens and pulls on the tendon, making the bone move. Stronger muscles make it much easier to move the skeleton.

Muscles are made up of individual muscle cells (muscle fibers) connected in bundles (fasciculi). Muscle fibers are composed of subunits called myofibrils (Figure 2–1). The covering of the entire muscle is called the epimysium; the covering of the fasciculi is called the perimysium; and muscle cells are covered by the endomysium. A sarcomere is an individual unit of muscle fibril. The myobrils are divided into units called myofilaments (actin and myosin), which slide across each other to cause muscle contraction (Figure 2–2). One of the goals of our weight training program is to increase the size of muscle fibers by increasing myofibrils. This process of enlarging muscle fibers is called **hypertrophy**. Generally, larger muscles tend to be stronger.

Does strength training enlarge the muscle fibers — or increase their number? This point has been argued for almost a hundred years. The bulk of evidence suggests that training makes muscle fibers larger (hypertrophy), not more numerous (**hyperplasia**). However, there is some proof that muscle fibers can increase in number under certain circumstances. Also, some extremely strong people may be born with more muscle fibers than others. Generally, though, it is muscle hypertrophy that makes muscles stronger.

Figure 2–1 Components of skeletal muscle tissue: fasciculi, muscle fiber, myofibrils, and myofilaments.

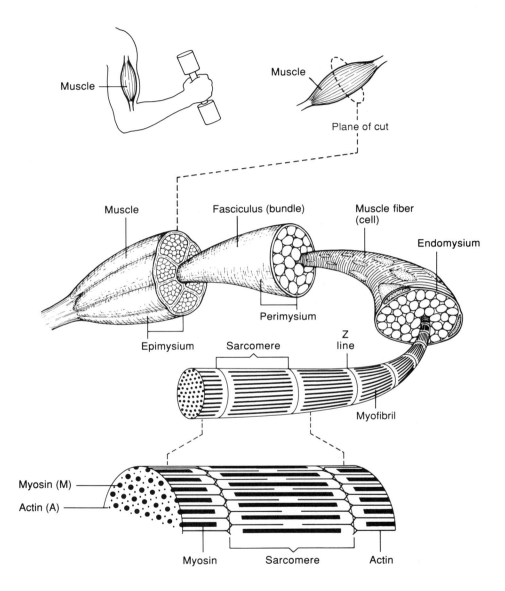

Figure 2–2 The sliding filament theory of muscle contraction. The myosin filaments pull on the actin filaments causing the muscle fiber to shorten. The basic contractile unit of the muscle fiber is the sarcomere. The Z membrane serves as the outer boundary of the sarcomere.

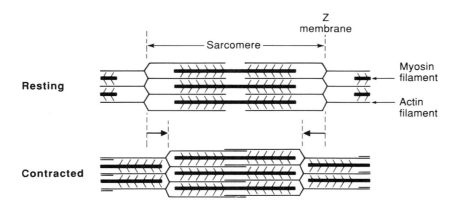

The Motor Unit

Muscle fibers receive the signal to contract from nerves connected to the spinal column. A motor nerve (a nerve connected to muscle fibers) may be linked to as few as one or two muscle fibers or to more than a hundred and fifty muscle fibers. Nerve-muscle combinations are called **motor units** (Figure 2–3). Powerful muscles, such as the quadriceps in the legs, have large motor units—each motor nerve is connected to many muscle fibers. Smaller muscles, such as those found around the eye, have much smaller motor units.

The three types of motor units are fast glycolytic (FG), fast oxidative glycolytic (FOG), and slow oxidative (SO). They are subdivided according to their strength and speed of contraction, speed of nerve conduction, and resistance to fatigue. The type of motor unit chosen by the body depends on the requirements of the activity. The body chooses FG fibers for lifting heavy weights or sprinting because these muscles are fast and powerful. However, SO fibers are chosen for prolonged standing or slow walking because they are more resistant to fatigue.

The body exerts force by calling on one or more motor units to contract. This process is called **motor unit recruitment**. When you want to pick up a small weight, for example, your body recruits a few motor units to do the task. However, when you want to pick up a large weight, you will use many motor units. When a motor unit calls upon its fibers to contract, all the fibers contract to their maximum capacity.

Increased strength through improved motor unit recruitment   Strength training improves your nervous system's ability to coordinate the recruitment of muscle fibers. It is a kind of ''muscle learning'' and is an important way of increasing strength. Because women

Figure 2–3 The motor unit. The motor unit is composed of a motor nerve and a number of muscle fibers.

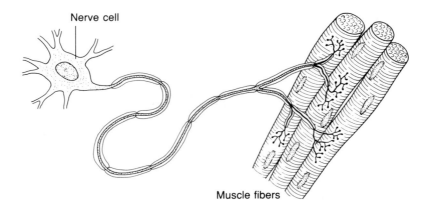

Nerve cell

Muscle fibers

don't have the same capacity for increasing muscle size as men, improved recruitment is essential. Muscles can increase in strength without greatly increasing in size and, in fact, most of the changes in strength during the first weeks of a weight training program are due to neurological adaptations. Table 2–1 summarizes some of the ways your body improves its function through weight training.

In summary, weight training increases muscle strength both by increasing the size of muscle fibers and by improving the body's ability to call on motor units to exert force. The first process is called muscle hypertrophy, and the second process is called motor unit recruitment.

Weight Training and the Strength of Ligaments, Tendons, and Bones

Tendons connect muscle to bone, and **ligaments** connect bones to other bones. Both tissues have little or no blood supply, so they heal slowly when injured. Scientists have found that these structures can be strengthened through exercise. This is fortunate, because when you develop stronger muscles through weight training, you run faster, lift more weight, and jump higher — placing more stress on the **joints**. But the body can easily tolerate increased loads because the tendons and ligaments are also strengthened.

WEIGHT TRAINING AND YOUR HEALTH

There are several conditions that are specific to or particularly important to women. These include amenorrhea, dysmenorrhea, premenstrual syndrome (PMS), incontinence, osteoporosis, kneecap pain, and pregnancy. It is important to know the effects of weight training on each of these. Problems related to diet, such as obesity, anorexia, and bulimia, will be discussed in chapter 11.

TABLE 2–1
Changes to the Body from Weight Training

CHANGE	EFFECT
Increased muscle mass	Tighter, firmer-looking body and stronger muscles
Increased size of fast-glycolytic muscle fibers	Increased muscle strength and power
Increased blood supply (high repetition program)	Increased delivery of oxygen and nutrients to the cells and increased elimination of wastes from the cells
Increased fuel storage in muscles	Increased resistance of muscles to fatigue
Ability to use more motor units during muscle contraction	Increased strength and power
Improved coordination of motor units	Increased strength and power
Increased strength of tendons, ligaments, and bone	Lower risk of injury to these tissues

Amenorrhea

Amenorrhea is the absence of menstruation. **Oligomenorrhea**, a related problem, is menstrual irregularity. Women who participate in extremely vigorous exercise have a higher incidence of these problems than do sedentary women.

CAUTION   ◆   Amenorrhea can have a variety of causes. If this is a persistent problem, see your physician.

Serious runners (i.e., women who run more than twenty to thirty miles per week) are very susceptible to menstrual irregularity. The chance of missed or late periods increases with miles run per week and the intensity of exercise. However, women runners who experience absent or irregular menses tend to have had the problem before they started running. So, the role of exercise is not entirely understood.

Amenorrhea among women body builders has been reported, but it is difficult to determine the exact cause of the problem. These women typically train very hard, consume low-calorie diets (before body building contests), have low body fat, and are under emotional stress. Each of these factors has been related to menstrual irregularity, so it's difficult to assess the role of weight training in the problem.

The phases of the normal twenty-eight-day menstrual cycle are controlled by the interaction of hormones, such as estrogen and progesterone. Levels of these hormones are low in women with abnormal menstrual cycles. Intense exercise has been identified as one factor that depresses these hormones.

What are the consequences of irregular or absent menstrual periods? Infertility (the inability to get pregnant) is associated with low female hormone levels during the second half of the menstrual cycle. Some evidence also suggests an increased risk of breast cancer in women with low progesterone levels. A surprising finding is that athletic women with irregular periods have reduced bone density and an increased risk of muscle and joint injury. This is interesting because exercise is usually associated with increased bone density. The causes of decreased bone density in women with amenorrhea are unknown, but many experts believe that low estrogen levels and inadequate dietary calcium may be important factors.

Experts at the gynecology center of the Georgetown School of Medicine Sports recommend that athletic women with irregular or absent menstrual periods get a medical examination. This should include a pelvic exam and appropriate hormonal blood tests. Menstrual irregularity can have many causes, ranging from pregnancy to failure of the ovaries. If you have this problem, it would be wise to get a medical checkup.

Dysmenorrhea

Dysmenorrhea is painful menstruation. It is caused by substances secreted by the inner lining of the uterus (womb) called **prostaglandins**. Prostaglandins make the blood vessels of the uterus contract, which causes pain. There are many drugs available that block prostaglandins and prevent or reduce pain. They make weight training bearable during a painful menstrual period. Many of these drugs are available only by prescription, but some, such as aspirin and Ibuprofen (e.g., Advil), are available over the counter. Dysmenorrhea can also be related to more serious conditions, such as endometriosis, and should not be ignored.

Premenstrual Syndrome

Premenstrual syndrome (PMS) usually affects women three to five days before the beginning of the menstrual period. Women with PMS may experience extreme anxiety, depression, mood swings, headaches, and water retention. The exact cause of PMS is unknown, but it is thought to be caused by hormonal changes during the menstrual cycle. If you have a severe PMS problem, you may want to ask your physician to prescribe medications that may help alleviate it.

Exercise has been shown to reduce the symptoms of PMS. Some researchers think it may be the natural ''high'' associated with exercise that improves the situation. Weight training, because of its positive effects on physiology and self-image, may help relieve PMS.

Incontinence

Incontinence (involuntary urinary leakage) can happen during weight training when pressure inside the abdomen exceeds the pressure preventing release of urine from the bladder. This condition can happen to any woman, but it is most common in those who have recently had a baby or who suffer from various anatomical defects.

There are several things you can do to prevent incontinence during your weight training routine. Avoid fluids for three hours before your workout, and empty your bladder before going into the weight room. Don't hold your breath, and try not to strain too hard when doing lifts. (Straining will increase intra-abdominal pressure and possibly urine leakage.) Do **Kegel exercises** regularly. These involve tightening the muscles in your **pelvis** that stop urine flow. Lastly, wear a mini-pad to diminish the chance of embarrassment and discomfort.

Osteoporosis

Decreases in bone mass, a condition called **osteoporosis**, is a serious health problem in women. Although the problem is most common in women who have reached menopause, recent evidence suggests that even active women in their twenties are susceptible. The causes of decreased bone density in women are complex and involve an interaction of hormonal controls, diet, and mechanical stress. Many studies have been done in recent years that suggest weight training may be an important activity for preventing osteoporosis.

CAUTION ◆ If you have reached the age of menopause, exercise alone may not be the most appropriate treatment for preventing osteoporosis. See your doctor for proper medical advice.

Bone density is, to some degree, proportional to the stresses placed on the bones. Studies show that active people have denser bones than sedentary people. This holds true for women with normal estrogen levels. If estrogen levels are normal and dietary intake of calcium adequate, then weight training will probably increase bone density. If estrogen levels and dietary calcium are low, then weight training will be less effective in maintaining bone mass. This appears to be true in adult women of any age.

Kneecap Pain

Women are more susceptible to kneecap pain than men because of their larger Q angle (Figure 2–4). The Q angle is formed by the axis of the femur (thigh bone) and the axis of the patellar ligament (the ligament connecting the kneecap to the tibia). The wider pelvis in women tends to draw the kneecap to the outside (laterally) of the joint, putting increased pressure on the underside of the kneecap. If your kneecaps hurt when you sit for prolonged periods — in your car, a movie theater, a classroom — you should be very careful not to make the problem worse. Weight training can either help or hurt.

Figure 2–4 The Q angle is formed by the axis of the femur and the axis of the patellar ligament. A wide Q angle causes the kneecap to be pulled outward. This may irritate the underside of the kneecap and cause knee pain.

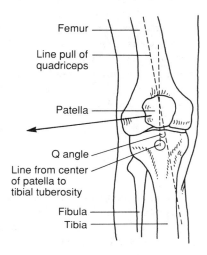

CAUTION ◆ Some weight training exercises, such as knee extensions, squats, and leg presses, may make kneecap pain worse. Check with a sports orthopedic physician or physical therapist if you are unsure which exercises are appropriate for you.

If you have kneecap pain, avoid any exercise that puts excess pressure on the joint. Examples include walking down stairs or hills, knee extensions, and full squats. Try to build up the muscle on the inside of your thigh. Appropriate exercises are shown in chapter 9. Try to keep your hamstring muscles (on the back of the thigh) as flexible as possible. Flexible hamstrings reduce pressure on the kneecap.

Pregnancy

Until recently pregnant women in most Western countries were advised to be sedentary. It is now recognized that, to a point, exercise is beneficial for most women during pregnancy. So it is no longer uncommon to see pregnant women in weight rooms, in swimming pools, and at running tracks.

CAUTION ◆ Always consult your obstetrician before beginning an exercise program during pregnancy.

The biggest concern when a pregnant woman exercises is injury to the fetus (unborn baby). Fetal injury can be caused by head compression, increased body temperature, decreased placental blood flow (the placenta transfers nutrients and oxygen from the mother's bloodstream to the fetus), and umbilical cord compression. Each of these problems can happen when a pregnant woman exercises. Another major problem is the distribution of blood between the working muscles of the pregnant woman and the unborn baby. During intense exercise, the baby could get shortchanged.

Happily, few problems have been reported among women who exercise during pregnancy. However, the possibility of tragedy is real. The key to avoiding problems is moderation. Don't hold your breath when you lift weights. Don't use too much weight or add more repetitions. Too much resistance may excessively increase blood pressure and intra-abdominal pressure. Lastly, don't exercise too intensely or for too long. For most pregnant women, the recommended exercising heart rate is between 135 and 150 beats per minute for a maximum of 25 minutes.

Even if you have not exercised before, you can begin a program during pregnancy, if the exercise is not too intense. Leading obstetricians who study exercise during pregnancy recommend that in previously sedentary women, the intensity of exercise not be increased until the second trimester (beginning month four).

References

Brooks, G. A., and T. D. Fahey. 1984. *Exercise physiology: Human bioenergetics and its applications*. New York: Macmillan.

Fahey, T. D. 1987. *Athletic training: Principles and practice*. Mtn. View, Calif.: Mayfield Publishing Co.

Gonyea, W. J., and D. Sale. 1982. "Physiology of weight lifting." *Arch. Phys. Med. Rehabil.* 63: 235–37.

Moritani, T., and H. A. deVries. 1979. "Neural factors versus hypertrophy in the time course of muscle strength gain." *Amer. J. Phys. Med.* 58: 115–30.

Morton, M. J., M. S. Paul, and J. Metcalf. 1985. "Exercise during pregnancy: Symposium on medical aspects of exercise." *Med. Clin. N. Amer.* 69: 97–108.

Mullinax, K. M., and E. Dale. 1986. "Some considerations of exercise during pregnancy." *Clinics Sports Med.* 5: 559–70.

Puhl, J. L., and C. H. Brown. 1986. *The menstrual cycle and physical activity*. Champaign, Ill.: Human Kinetics Publishers.

Sale, D. G. 1988. "Neural adaptations to resistance training." *Med. Sci. Sports Exerc.* 20: S135–S145.

Sanborn, C. F., B. J. Martin, and W. W. Wagner. 1982. "Is athletic amenorrhea specific to runners?" *Am. J. Obstet. Gynecol.* 143: 859–66.

Shangold, M., and G. Mirkin. 1988. *Women and exercise: Physiology and sports medicine*. Philadelphia: F. A. Davis Co.

Wells, C. L. 1985. *Women, sport and performance*. Champaign, Ill.: Human Kinetics Publishers.

3 Basic Principles of Weight Training

THE HUMAN BODY IS A REMARKABLE ORGANISM BECAUSE IT ADAPTS TO THE PHYSICAL requirements of daily life. If you are required to lift heavy objects regularly, then your muscles get stronger. But if you seldom do any exercise, then your muscles will be small, reflecting your sedentary life-style.

Weight training can be an important tool for developing the kind of body you want. This activity will increase muscle tone and size and will give you a lean, smooth, athletic look. If you combine weight training with a good diet and aerobic workout, you can almost guarantee progress toward your ultimate goal.

Weight training works best when you have a plan. The plan helps you make progress in small steps that bring you closer and closer to your eventual goal. The training principles we present are very simple, but guaranteed to bring results if followed faithfully.

When you train, you are acting very much like a doctor who works to cure a disease. You administer a treatment (for example, a workout involving weight training, swimming, or running) to change the body's functioning (to improve fitness). When you train with weights, you're stimulating your body to improve communications between nerves and muscles. You're getting the muscles to make more protein, which makes them stronger and improves their tone. Through training, you are compelling your body to adapt to increased demands and to improve its ability to function.

Your training program should be designed to increase fitness and prevent injury. (See the discussion of stress adaptation in chapter 4 and Figure 4–1.) Every time you plan a workout, ask yourself this question: "Is this exercise session going to help my body improve its functioning?" The answer won't always be yes. Sometimes rest is more appropriate than exercise, or a less intense workout is sometimes better than an exhausting one. The basic purpose of a workout is to introduce a stress you can adapt to, but not one so severe that you break down.

To get the most from your weight training program, we recommend the following **thirteen principles of training**. These principles are a guide to gradual and long-lasting fitness development and will lead to improved performance with the smallest risk of injury.

1. Train the way you want your body to change. This means stress your body so that it produces the changes you want. If you are primarily concerned with general fitness, choose a well-rounded program that concentrates on the major muscle groups. Besides your weight training routine, your program should include endurance and flexibility exercises. Weight training alone will not develop all-around physical fitness.

    If you are a body builder, work on your weaknesses, even if the exercises necessary to correct them are unpleasant. For example, if you are a skier, having strong, flexible lower body muscles is more important than having strong arms and shoulders. Analyze what you're doing. A well-designed program will be more effective and less time-consuming.

2. Eat a well-balanced, high-performance diet. During the past twenty years, sports scientists have shown that the right diet can improve performance and keep off unwanted pounds of fat. All the training in the world will not give you a great body if you eat too much. Eat a sensible, nutritious diet (one containing a balance of the basic food groups). The diet should supply enough calories to meet your energy needs but still allow you to control your weight. If you want to lose weight, do so gradually, no more than two and a half pounds per week. If you are training hard, eat more carbohydrates and fewer fats.

3. Train all year round. If you take off too much time from your exercise program, you will lose the gains you've made. And you'll be more susceptible to injury if you try to get back in shape rapidly. Establish a year-round program; have specific goals and procedures for each period of the year — and stick to them.

    Make sure you have alternative training plans for when the weather is bad or you don't have access to a weight room. For example, if you are on a trip, substitute calisthenics exercises — such as push-ups and knee bends — for your regular routine. Set aside a certain part of the day for your exercise routine to make sure you get that workout. Your exercise time is the part of the day that belongs to you alone — don't let anyone take it away.

4. Get in shape gradually. Training is a stress the body must overcome, so give your body time to adapt to the stress of exercise. Muscles are more susceptible to injury during the early phases of conditioning. Overzealous training, or intense conditioning when you aren't prepared for it, will lead to injury and delay progress.

    Staying in good shape all year long is much easier than trying to achieve fitness in a few months. It's much easier to apply a little pressure instead of trying to go for a crash conditioning program.

5. Don't train when you're ill or seriously injured. The body has problems trying to fight more than one stressor at a time. Training when you are sick or injured may seriously hinder your progress or even be dangerous. It is particularly important not to train when you have a fever.

    After an injury, you can return to intense workouts if you can answer yes to these questions.

    ◆ Can you move the injured area (joint, muscle, etc.) normally?

    ◆ Do you have normal strength and power?

    ◆ Have normal movement patterns been restored (more than 90 percent recovered)?

    ◆ Are you relatively pain-free?

    If the answer to any of these questions is no, then you should let the injury heal further (through a combination of rehabilitation and rest) or modify your program as long as necessary. Many people end up abandoning their favorite sports because of injuries that were not allowed to heal properly. Dealing effectively with injuries is just as important as having a well-designed training program.

6. Train first for volume (more repetitions) and only later for intensity (more weight or resistance). Soft tissues, such as muscle, tendons, and ligaments, take a long time to adjust to the rigors of training. If your goal is to get as strong as possible, begin your program by doing more repetitions, not adding weight. This will prevent injury, strengthen your body gradually, and prepare it for heavy training. During later training sessions, when you're in shape, you can use more weight and fewer repetitions to increase strength at a faster rate. If your goal is to have good muscle tone and muscular endurance, you may always want to emphasize repetitions rather than weight.

7. Listen to your body. Don't stick to your planned program too stubbornly if it doesn't feel right. Sometimes your body needs rest more than it needs exercise. Most studies show that the absolute **intensity** is the essential factor in improving fitness. Typically, an overtrained person has not recovered enough to train at an optimal intensity; so, a few days of rest may be necessary to allow the body to recover enough to resume intense training. **Overtraining** is a condition characterized by fatigue, decreased performance, irritability, and sometimes depression.

    Be consistent in your training. If you listen to your body and it always tells you to rest, you won't make any progress. You have to work hard to improve your fitness significantly. It is essential to try to maintain a structured workout program. If you never feel like training hard, it may be that you have a medical problem or you lack motivation.

8. Vary the volume and intensity of your workouts. This technique is sometimes called **periodization** or **cycle training**. It allows the body to recover when it needs to and to train hard when hard training is called for.

The principle is simple: you do a particular exercise more intensely in one workout than in another rather than training at maximum intensity for every exercise during every weight training session.

Although sophisticated workout cycles are most suitable for athletes, women interested in general fitness can also benefit from cycle training because it allows the body to adapt and become stronger more rapidly. If your goal is to improve muscle tone and body composition (the proportion of fat and fat-free weight), you can benefit from cycle training also. Try varying the exercises in your workouts. For example, instead of doing bench presses three days a week, substitute incline presses one day. Cycle training makes working out with weights more interesting and helps you to progress faster. (Cycle training is discussed in more detail in chapter 5.)

9. Don't overtrain. This principle is difficult to stick to because it opposes the work ethic that is ingrained in so many of us. Think of conditioning as a long-term process. Adaptations to training happen gradually. Too much training tends to lead to overtraining and overuse injuries, not faster development of fitness.

Learn to recognize the signs of overtraining. Some of these include fatigue, muscle soreness and weakness, irritability, lack of motivation, insomnia, depression, increased proneness to illness. When you are overtrained, you must reexamine your training program and diet. Usually more rest and a high-performance diet will help. (See chapter 11 for a detailed discussion of diet.)

10. Train systematically. Plan a proper workout schedule for the coming months, but don't be so rigid that you can't change the program to fit unforeseen circumstances. The important thing is that you have a plan, so you can comfortably apply the stress of exercise in a manner that will produce a consistent increase in fitness.

A coach, a training partner, and a training diary will help you become more systematic. A good coach or instructor, who is knowledgeable and experienced, can keep you from making common mistakes and help motivate you to meet your fitness goals. For people who need a little more motivation and have the money, a personal trainer — who works with you during your workout — may be a way to make rapid gains.

A training partner is important for motivation and safety. It is a lot easier to make it to your workout if you are accountable to someone. Your partner can encourage you and help **spot** you when you need help (a spotter assists you during the exercise). He or she will share the agony and ecstasy that accompanies training.

Writing down what you hope to achieve in a training diary or workout card will also help you attain your fitness goals. Use your diary to keep track of which techniques work for you and which don't. A sample workout card is attached to the cover of this book.

11. Train your mind. One of the most difficult skills to acquire — but critical for attaining high levels of physical fitness — is mind control. Training the mind is thoroughly interrelated with training the body — you can achieve almost anything if you set your mind to it. To become physically fit or to succeed as an athlete, you must believe in yourself and your potential, have goals, and know how to achieve these goals. It requires discipline and is an ongoing process. You must be able to put yourself in the proper frame of mind in order to do this.

12. Learn all you can about exercise. If you know why the various components of training are important, you are much more likely to plan an intelligent, effective program. You will be less liable to jump into every training fad that comes along, and you will always be in control of your own program. Being informed, you'll buy better and more economical sports equipment, manage many of your own athletic injuries, and have a more efficient training routine. Learn everything you can about training, and you will get the most from your exercise program.

13. Keep the exercise program in its proper perspective. Too often, the exercise program takes on inappropriate importance in a person's life. Some women think of themselves almost solely as aerobic dancers, runners, triathletes, or swimmers, rather than as human beings who participate in those activities. While exercise is important, you must also have time for other aspects of your life. Leading a well-rounded life will not diminish your chances for success and will make your training program more enjoyable.

WEIGHT TRAINING AS PART OF THE TOTAL FITNESS PROGRAM

Exercise training is an attempt to mold your body to improve it. Your body changes according to the way you stress it. If you work your muscles to exert more force than they are used to, they get stronger. If you exercise for extended periods, your endurance improves. You can tailor your program to develop the kind of fitness you want.

Determining Your Goals

There are many weight training exercises and programs. The right one for you depends on your goals. For example, if your goal is to have a healthy-looking body, your program will be different than if you want to improve fitness for sports. Whatever your ultimate goal, it is best to begin the program doing many repetitions (10–15 repetitions) before trying heavy loads. Specific programs for a variety of program goals appear in appendix 2.

Developing an Attractive, Healthy-looking Body

Most everyone wants a healthy-looking body, but this often seems like an impossible goal. No matter how many sit-ups, leg lifts, and twists we do, many of us can't seem to get rid of those unwanted bulges. Let's face it, having a dynamite body is no easy task. Much of the problem stems from misinformation and unrealistic expectations about the methods and benefits of weight training. There are several basic principles for women interested in developing a lean, athletic-looking body.

The first principle is to **reduce body fat**. Weight training alone won't do it! Discussed in detail in chapter 11, the control of body fat is determined by an energy balance: if more energy (food) is consumed than is expended (metabolism and exercise), then fat is gained; conversely, fat is lost when energy expenditure exceeds energy intake. Body fat may be controlled by eating a well-balanced diet containing adequate but not excessive calories (energy) and by participating in aerobic exercise in addition to weight training.

CAUTION   ◆   Don't try to improve the appearance of your body through weight training alone. Weight training should be part of a general program that includes a sensible diet and aerobic exercise.

Weight training mainly affects your muscles, which are covered by a layer of fat and skin. Increasing strength and muscle tone will do little to give you the lean look you want if the muscles are covered by a thick layer of fat. Weight training *will* improve the appearance of your body if you lose fat gradually, don't develop too much loose skin, and gain muscle mass. Then the increased size of the muscles gives your body a leaner, more attractive shape.

Although it has only a small effect on the energy balance that controls fat, weight training by itself can improve the appearance of certain parts of the body, particularly the abdomen, to some degree. The exercises increase muscle tone, which makes the body part look tighter — but the fat will stay unless you shift the general energy balance. There is no such thing as spot reducing: you cannot lose fat in a specific area of the body by exercising the nearby muscles.

The second principle is to build muscle size using high-intensity exercise. As discussed in chapter 2, it is more difficult for women to gain muscle mass than men. However, if they train intensely enough (i.e., use heavy enough weights), women can develop larger muscles. Muscles get bigger when subjected to heavy loads (that is, high muscle tension) during training. If you build muscle as well as lose fat, you will get a better-looking body.

Body builders often overemphasize workouts involving many repetitions and many sets (a repetition is one performance of the exercise; a set is a group of repetitions followed by rest). Although these workouts are essential for defining muscle shape, they are less effective for developing muscle size. So, for women who want to increase muscle size, some high-intensity training should be in the program. Women who don't want to increase muscle bulk should do more repetitions and use less weight.

CAUTION   ◆   If you want to prevent excessive muscle bulk but tend to put on much muscle tissue when you weight train, avoid low-repetition–high-resistance exercises. Instead, do more repetitions and use less weight.

The third principle for developing a healthy-looking body is to **develop muscle definition**. Muscle definition is the elusive property of muscles that allows their structure to be defined and seen more clearly. For example, legs look a lot better when defined muscle gives them more shape. The way to muscle definition is through high-set, high-repetition workouts. However, high numbers of repetitions and sets are of limited value in improving muscle definition if you have too much body fat.

Improving Strength for Other Activities

The body changes from an exercise program according to the stresses placed upon it. Each sport or physical activity has specific physical demands. Skiers need strong leg muscles with plenty of endurance. Golfers need strong forearm, back, and leg muscles. The weight training routine must be structured to meet the needs of the sport.

It is also important to focus on muscles and joints commonly injured in sports. For example, many women swimmers and tennis players get shoulder injuries ("rotator cuff"). Unfortunately, these muscles are seldom conditioned in loosely structured weight training programs — until they are injured. It makes a lot more sense to precondition vulnerable joints and muscles to prevent injury.

There are three major weight training principles for increasing strength for sports and daily physical activities:

♦ Identify and train those muscles and joints particularly important in the activity.

♦ Identify and train those muscles and joints prone to injury in the activity.

♦ Maintain a good level of fitness in the major muscle groups of the body.

Developing Strength and Power

More and more women are interested in building strength for its own sake, and there are weight lifting competitions for women in power and Olympic lifting. Power lifting involves **maximum lifts** in the bench press, squat, and dead lift. Olympic lifting includes the clean and jerk and snatch. Many women are also interested in improving strength for strength-speed sports, such as track and field.

The weight training programs for women who want to improve fitness for strength-speed sports center on three types of weight lifting exercises: presses, pulls, and multijoint lower body exercises. Presses include the bench press, incline press, military press, seated press, push press, jerks, and dumbbell press. Pulls include cleans, snatches, high pulls, and dead lifts. Multijoint lower body exercises include squats, leg presses, hack squats, and rack squats.

Generally, heavy loads (loads weighing 70–100 percent of your maximum lifting capacity) and a low to moderate number of repetitions (1–8 times) are used to gain maximum strength and power. Supporting exercises to develop arm, back, abdominal, calf, and neck muscle strength (depending on the sport) are also practiced. But presses, pulls, and multijoint lower body exercises form the core of the program.

TABLE 3–1
The Principles of Weight Training

- Train the way you want your body to change.
- Eat a well-balanced, high-performance diet.
- Train all year round.
- Get in shape gradually.
- Don't train when you're ill or seriously injured.
- Train first for volume (increasing repetitions) and only later for intensity (increasing weight or resistance).
- Listen to your body.
- Vary (cycle) the volume and intensity of your workouts.
- Don't overtrain.
- Train systematically.
- Train your mind.
- Learn all you can about exercise.
- Keep the exercise program in its proper perspective.

Strength–speed athletes hold a variety of training philosophies. Traditionally, programs often involved training three days per week, using as much weight as possible for each lift. Each workout was the same. Now, new ideas have hit the scene. Athletes and coaches have found that doing all three types of strength–speed exercises during each workout hinders recovery, leads to overtraining, and delays progress. Cycle training, in which volume and intensity of exercises are varied from workout to workout and at different times of the year, speeds up progress. (Cycle training will be described in greater detail in chapter 5.)

WEIGHT TRAINING AS PART OF A GENERAL CONDITIONING PROGRAM

Fitness has many components, including endurance, strength, power, speed, agility, flexibility, balance, and absence of disease. Each of these components is developed in a particular way in each sport or physical activity. For example, a woman may have excellent endurance on a ski slope but poor endurance on the running track or in the swimming pool. So, to be fit for a variety of physical activities, you have to practice those activities. Regular participation in weight, flexibility, and endurance training will carry over into most of the activities of daily life and improve your performance.

It is almost impossible to stay optimally fit for all the activities you enjoy. Only Superwoman could do regular conditioning exercises, ski, hike, swim, play tennis and volleyball, golf, and windsurf several times a week while also working or attending school. You must make compromises. It is better to choose a few exercises to do regularly than to choose an overambitious program that cannot be maintained. A general conditioning program, designed to prepare you for an active life-style and foster good health, should contain the following components:

◆ Endurance exercise. The most essential part of any conditioning program is endurance exercise because it affects the heart and circulation and helps prevent heart disease. A general endurance exercise plan is to do large-muscle endurance activities — such as running, walking, cycling, or swimming — three to five times per week at over 50 percent of your maximum capacity (70 percent of maximum heart rate) for twenty to sixty minutes. Note that 50 percent effort results in a heart rate that is approximately 70 percent of the maximum heart rate.

◆ Flexibility exercise. Flexibility, or stretching, exercises are important for maintaining the normal range of motion of the major joints of the body. These exercises should be done at least five times per week. A minimal program should include stretches for the hamstrings (back of the thigh), quadriceps (front of the thigh), Achilles tendons, groin (inside of the thigh), back, and shoulders. Stretches should be practiced statically (stretch and hold), never stretching to the point of pain in the muscle.

CAUTION   ◆   Never "bounce" during stretching exercise.

◆ Weight training. A basic weight training program should be practiced two to four days per week, working the major muscle groups. The program should include exercises for the shoulders, chest, arms, abdomen, back, and legs. Workouts should last thirty to sixty minutes.

◆ Sports or physical activities you enjoy. Conditioning is much easier if it is part of an activity you like to do. For example, aerobics and swimming are terrific conditioning activities, which many women find more enjoyable than running. Cross-country skiing is a great exercise to substitute for more traditional endurance exercises when you are on vacation. Tennis, racquetball, basketball, and soccer provide a good conditioning effect and can be used to supplement the exercise program. Sports skills are valuable because they often contribute to all the components of fitness and tend to be more fun than exercises devised merely for conditioning.

Be as active as you can be. Participate in as many activities as time allows, but don't get stuck in a rut or overemphasize only one component of fitness. Too many people either weight train or run, forgetting about the other areas of fitness. If your goal is to attain a healthy, attractive body, capable of doing many activities, you are better off participating in several types of exercise (endurance, strength, and flexibility) than concentrating on only one.

4 How Weight Training Improves Your Body

WEIGHT TRAINING IS MUCH LIKE A SAVINGS ACCOUNT TO WHICH YOU ADD A SMALL amount of money each week. The money from any weekly deposit will not make you rich, but the accumulated effect of many small deposits can add up to a lot of money. A single weight training session will not improve fitness very much. However, if you add the effects of months of training, improvements will be substantial.

As with any human activity, weight training has its own language. Words like ''reps'' (repetitions), ''sets,'' ''PRs'' (personal records), ''max'' (maximum), ''burn,'' and ''pump'' are all part of the jargon of weight training. A basic understanding of weight training expressions is necessary so you can understand what other lifters are talking about.

STRESS ADAPTATION

When the body is subjected to a **stress** such as exercise, it either **adapts** or breaks down. You get injured when your body can't handle the stress. (See Figure 4–1.) The purpose of a training program is to subject the body to a physical stress to which it can adapt—not a stress so severe that it causes the body injury. Every time you walk into the weight room you should ask yourself this question: ''Will this workout help my body to adapt and become stronger?'' Sometimes you will have to train harder to accelerate the rate of adaptation. At other times you will need to rest to get the most from your program.

Figure 4–1 Stress adaptation. Some exercise stress causes improved fitness, but excessive stress causes injury.

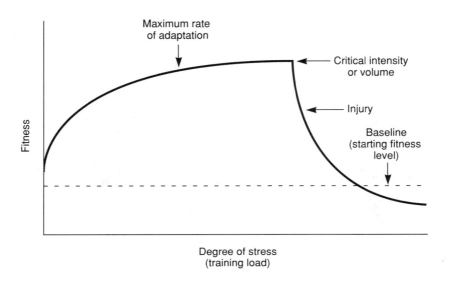

Overload

The basis of stress adaptation is overload, which exposes the body to more stress than it is used to. The components of overload are load, repetition, rest, and frequency. Each factor affects the others. For example, if load is high, then repetitions are usually lower and rest is longer.

Load is the intensity of exercise, the amount of resistance or weight used during the movement. Generally, the greater the load, the faster you fatigue and the longer it takes to recover. Of all the components of overload, load is probably the most important for gaining strength. High loads lead to the fastest improvements in strength and muscle size. If you find you are gaining more muscle mass than you want, keep the load down and increase repetitions.

A repetition is one performance of an exercise. A set is a group of repetitions followed by rest. Adaptation tends to happen more quickly when an exercise is done more than once. Beginners should initially use 10–12 repetitions for 2–3 sets per exercise. After two to three weeks of training, do 3 sets per exercise, with the same number of repetitions, but use more weight. Advanced routines will include between 1 and 15 repetitions, depending on the purpose of the training program.

Rest is the time between sets. Rest is vitally important for adaptation and should be used according to the desired result. For example, a weight lifter who wants maximum strength is most concerned with load and therefore needs a considerable amount of rest between exercises. But a runner is more concerned with muscular **endurance** (the ability to sustain prolonged muscular exercise), so she would take shorter rests between sets.

Frequency is the number of training sessions per week. Most people who train with weights do so three times per week, but frequency may vary between two and five times per week. People who train with weights four to five times per week typically emphasize specific muscle groups during a workout. For example, they might exercise lower body muscle groups on Monday and Thursday and upper body muscles on Tuesday and Saturday.

Frequency of training must be determined according to the desired result. Although intense training programs can improve performance in many sports, this kind of workout must be tempered with proper recovery periods, or injury may result. More is not always better. Excessive training may also lead to overtraining, which will stall progress and lead to injury.

Consistency in training is also critical. Large gains are made in small steps. While overtraining is a problem for many people, inconsistency is the main problem for the average person. You have to do your exercise routine regularly if you are going to improve your fitness.

Specificity of Training

The body adapts specifically to the stress of exercise. In other words, the adaptation to endurance exercise (e.g., distance running or swimming) is different from the adaptation to strength exercise (e.g., weight training) or to power exercise (e.g., sprinting). Your training program and the exercises you choose should reflect the desired adaptation. The closer the training to the requirements of the sport, the more valuable will be the result. If you are weight training to get in shape for skiing, for example, then concentrate on lower body exercises. If you are interested in improving your appearance, then do more varied exercises, concentrating on those parts of the body that need work. Your body will adapt to the stresses you give it, so structure your program carefully — or you may end up with a result you don't want.

Individual Differences

We were not all created equal when it comes to body shape, strength, physical skill, and endurance. These differences determine how fast we learn sports skills, how we look in a bathing suit, and how we respond to an exercise program. Your ability to respond to an exercise program (weight training or any other type) depends on genetics as well as on the intensity of training. Both are important to performance.

Even a woman with a naturally well-defined body and good health will fail to get in top shape if she doesn't devote enough time and effort to training. On the other hand, a woman without genetic gifts of fitness may find it difficult to achieve superior levels of strength and body composition — even if she "kills" herself in the weight room.

Most of us fall somewhere in the middle between wonder woman and total klutz. A good training program can help you develop your potential and overcome your weaknesses. Even the weakest among us can get strong if the training program is intense enough. You can't expect to see miraculous changes overnight, but if you're patient and train consistently and correctly, you *will* attain the desired results.

Reversibility

"If you don't use it, you'll lose it." That's an old maxim of exercise training. The purpose of training, or any other type of exercise, is to stress the muscles more than usual to make them stronger and larger. But if less than normal stress is placed on the muscles, then the muscles **atrophy** (shrink) and get weaker. That's what happens when your broken leg is put in a plaster cast. In other words, gains made by training are **reversible**.

It is important to stay fit year-round. Maintaining fitness is much easier than regaining a level of conditioning you have lost. High levels of fitness and a great body call for many years of training and involve small stages of progression. The body can't be forced to adapt rapidly; an attempt to do so will only cause injury.

TYPES OF WEIGHT TRAINING EXERCISES

Women who weight train are interested in at least one of its three main effects on the body: (1) an increase in muscular strength, (2) an increase in muscular power, and (3) a change in muscular shape. **Strength** is the ability to exert force. **Power** is work per unit of time — in other words, power is the ability to exert force rapidly. In most sports, power is more important than strength. Fortunately, there is a transfer between strength and power — exercises that develop strength also tend to develop power.

Many women spend long hours developing strength in the weight room to increase power in sports. Tennis players, for example, often do bench presses or lat pulls to help them serve and hit the ball harder. The weights are lifted at much slower speeds than the racket is moved during a tennis match, yet the strength gained during the relatively slow exercises gives increased power in the faster tennis movements.

There are two kinds of strength exercises: **isometric** (static) and **isotonic** (dynamic). Isometric exercise involves applying force without movement; isotonic exercise is exerting force with movement. These exercises can be done concentrically or eccentrically. A **concentric muscle contraction** occurs when the muscle applies force as it shortens. This happens during the active phase of a weight training exercise. In an **eccentric muscle contraction**, force is exerted as the muscle lengthens. For example, it may begin when the weight is lowered to begin the pushing phase of the exercise.

Isometric Exercise

Isometric exercise is a static muscle contraction involving no movement. An immovable object, such as a fixed bar or wall, is used to provide resistance.

Although isometric exercise received considerable attention in the late 1950s, it is now less popular as a primary means of gaining strength. Isometric exercise does not increase strength throughout a joint's range of motion (unless practiced at various points in the range of motion); strength is gained only at or near the joint angle where the exercise is practiced. Also, isometric training does not improve (and may even hamper) the ability to exert force rapidly. Doing too much isometric training may lead to injury.

Weight trainers occasionally use isometrics to overcome "sticking points" in an exercise's range of motion. For example, people who have difficulty pushing weights from their chest during the bench press may do the exercise isometrically at the point where they are having the most difficulty. A **power rack** (Figure 4–2) is sometimes used for this type of isometric training.

You can also do isometric exercise without using anything for resistance. For example, you can simply tighten and release the abdominal muscles, a good way to tone and strengthen them. This type of exercise is especially valuable when recovering from an injury. It can be practiced almost anywhere and doesn't require any equipment. Examples of isometric exercises useful for strengthening the lower back and abdomen appear in chapters 8 and 9, respectively.

Electrical muscle stimulation (EMS)   EMS is a form of isometric exercise used by some people as a substitute for active movement. A small electrical charge is sent into the muscle, causing it to contract. EMS can build muscle strength and is particularly valuable for injured people who are not capable of active movement (e.g., following surgery). But beware of false claims that EMS is equal or superior to weight training or aerobic exercise. It has its place, but it is not suitable as a primary form of physical activity.

CAUTION   ◆   EMS can cause injury if applied incorrectly. If you are going to use this muscle-strengthening technique, be sure to receive proper training from your therapist or physician.

Figure 4–2   The power rack. This device is used to help overcome "sticking points." This exercise is the power rack squat.

Isotonic Exercise

Isotonic exercise involves muscle contractions that result in movement. The most common and popular type of weight training, isotonic exercises may involve weight machines, barbells, dumbbells, or the body's own weight (e.g., push-ups). Isotonic techniques include constant resistance, variable resistance, eccentric loading, plyometrics, speed loading, and isokinetic exercise.

Constant resistance   Constant resistance exercise uses a constant load, such as a barbell or dumbbell, throughout the range of motion. It is the most common form of weight training. Despite the fact that you are using a constant load (the same barbell or dumbbell) throughout the exercise, the *relative* resistance varies with the angle of the joint. So it is usually easier to move the weight at the end of the movement, where you have better leverage, than at the beginning. Maximum loading, therefore, occurs at the weakest point in the range of motion.

Variable resistance   Variable resistance exercise involves special weight machines that change the load throughout the range of motion so there is a more consistent stress on the muscles. Variable resistance machines place more stress on the muscles at the end of the range of motion, where you have better leverage and are capable of exerting more force.

Numerous variable resistance machines are on the market, including those made by Areal, Universal, Nautilus, Eagle, Marcy, and Kaiser. Sports scientists have not yet determined if this form of training is superior to constant resistance exercise. However, the machines are safe and easy to use, and they are extremely popular with many people.

Eccentric loading   As discussed above, **eccentric loading** occurs when the muscle lengthens while exerting force. Muscles contract eccentrically whenever a weight is lowered into position prior to lifting it. This type of contraction is vital in training because it allows you to control a weight. If your body were incapable of contracting muscles eccentrically, controlled movement would be impossible.

The active phase of most weight training exercises (lifting the weight) is concentric. However, exercises can also be performed solely eccentrically, a type of training popularly referred to as "negatives." Eccentric loading is an effective way to gain strength and a useful supplement to concentric exercises.

CAUTION   ◆   Eccentric exercise can cause extreme muscle soreness. Increase the volume and intensity of this type of exercise very gradually.

One drawback is that it seems to cause more muscle soreness than other methods. The high tension generated during this technique causes small tears in the muscle that result in muscle soreness a day or two after the workout. As with other forms of exercise, eccentric loading is useful only if not overdone.

Plyometrics   Plyometrics involves sudden eccentric loading and stretching of muscles followed by forceful concentric contraction. The sudden stretch stimulates receptors in the muscles and the muscles' own elasticity to react and cause a stronger contraction when they shorten. An example of plyometrics is jumping from a bench to the ground and then jumping back onto the bench (Figure 4–3).

CAUTION ◆ Plyometrics can cause injury if practiced excessively. Begin with only a few repetitions of these exercises, and increase the volume and intensity very gradually.

Plyometrics should be practiced to develop a specifically desired type of power. For example, to increase jumping power for volleyball, practice plyometrics in a vertical direction. To develop the shoulder muscles, lean against a wall at an angle of forty-five to sixty degrees. Push up forcefully, allow yourself to go back against the wall and absorb your fall with your arms, then immediately push off again (Figure 4–4).

Doing many repetitions of plyometrics will develop muscle strength and endurance. This form of exercise is particularly effective in improving communication between the muscles and nervous system (see the section entitled ''Muscle Structure and Strength'' in chapter 2) and has become very popular with many women.

Speed loading   Speed loading involves moving a weight as rapidly as possible in an attempt to approach the speeds used in movements such as throwing a softball or sprinting. For gaining strength, weight training at ordinary speeds is superior, because in speed loading the muscles are not sufficiently tensed to cause a training effect. Few studies have looked at how this type of exercise trains the nervous system. It may be effective in improving power (the ability to exert force rapidly).

Figure 4–3 Plyometrics. This type of isotonic exercise overloads the muscles' elastic component, which results in a forceful muscle contraction. The technique is practiced to improve strength and power. An exercise to develop leg power involves (a and b) jumping off a low bench, (c) landing on the floor and absorbing the shock with the legs, and (d) jumping back up onto the bench.

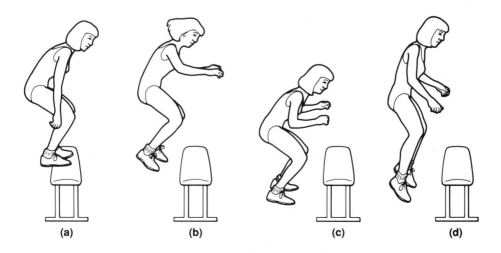

(a)   (b)   (c)   (d)

Figure 4–4 Upper body plyometrics.

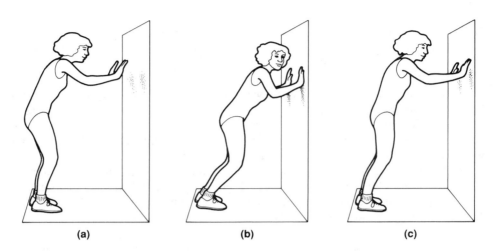

(a)   (b)   (c)

Isokinetic exercise   Also called "accommodating resistance exercise," **isokinetic** exercise involves muscle contraction at a constant speed. The exerted force is resisted by an equal force from the isokinetic machine. You feel resistance only when you're applying force. For this reason, isokinetics are considered safer than other forms of strength training. Isokinetic devices are used for strength training and measurement at fast speeds of movement.

Promoters of isokinetic strength training equipment say that the machines improve power, which is the type of strength needed in most sports. They are widely used by physical therapists for rehabilitating muscle and joint injuries. These machines tend to be considerably more expensive than traditional weight training equipment, so they are not as widely available.

Proprioceptive neuromuscular facilitation (PNF)   PNF is manual resistance exercise that combines stretching with isotonic and isometric exercise. This technique is widely used by physical therapists to develop strength and flexibility in injured patients. As yet, it is not commonly used by many women for improving physical fitness.

References

Brooks, G. A., and T. D. Fahey. 1984. *Exercise physiology: Human bioenergetics and its applications*. New York: Macmillan.

DeLorme, R., and F. Stransky. 1990. *Fitness and fallacies*. Dubuque, Iowa: Kendall/Hunt Publishing Co.

Fahey, T. D. 1987. *Athletic training: Principles and practice*. Mtn. View, Calif.: Mayfield Publishing Co.

Shangold, M., and G. Mirkin. 1988. *Women and exercise: Physiology and sports medicine*. Philadelphia: F. A. Davis Co.

C H A P T E R

5

Getting Started:
The Basics

STARTING A NEW TYPE OF EXERCISE PROGRAM IS A LOT LIKE MOVING TO A NEW TOWN — you feel awkward, and everything is new and strange. To begin weight training, you must first make some decisions: where to train, what clothes to wear, and which exercises to do. When you know the basics, you'll feel more at ease, your program will be safer and more enjoyable, and you'll be on the path to being an informed fitness consumer.

MEDICAL CHECKUP

Before beginning a program, you should determine if weight training is suitable for you. If you are under thirty-five years old and in good health, there is probably no reason not to enter a weight training program. If you are over thirty-five or have health problems — especially high blood pressure, heart disease, stroke, obesity, or musculoskeletal disorders — you should consult a physician before you start.

It is best to choose a physician who knows something about exercise. Find a doctor who likes to exercise or has training in exercise physiology or sports medicine. Physicians are required to stay current in their field by earning continuing medical education credits, and many physicians attend seminars in **sports medicine**. Local health clubs, university exercise physiology departments, and medical societies are often good sources for referrals to physicians with knowledge of sports medicine.

If you are over thirty-five or have significant health problems, beware of health clubs or fitness classes that offer fitness screening without proper medical supervision. Fitness evaluations by nonphysicians are not substitutes for a pretraining medical examination, and it could be dangerous to rely on them. Organizations such as the **American College of Sports Medicine** and the American Heart Association have established guidelines for fitness testing of adults and children. Make sure your club follows these guidelines.

CHOOSING A HEALTH CLUB OR WEIGHT TRAINING CLASS

Good health clubs and college weight rooms typically have expensive and specialized weight machines that will enhance your program. These machines help you safely isolate and develop specific muscle groups in the chest, arms, hips, buttocks, and legs. You don't have to worry about a mountain of weights falling on your head when you miss a repetition of an exercise. Instead, if a weight is too much or not enough for you, you simply move the weight pin from one place to another in the weight stack.

A club is also a great place to socialize. Many health spas have juice bars where you can meet new friends. Socializing helps to take the drudgery out of working out — it's a lot easier to sweat if you're doing it among friends.

Joining a health club allows you to get in some aerobic exercise too, saving you a trip to the track or pool. Most clubs have aerobics classes going almost constantly. It's easy to catch a class for forty or fifty minutes, then go to the weight room and finish your workout. If aerobics classes aren't for you, you can ride a stationary bike or train on a stair-climbing machine. Well-equipped clubs often have a running track, swimming pool, racquetball courts, or computerized rowing machines.

The following guidelines can help you to choose the right club. Making the wrong choice will lead to a frustrating and possibly very expensive mistake.

1. You should get value for your money.

   ◆ Be wary of signing up for a health club that does not yet exist. There have been many instances of clubs collecting money from potential members for facilities being built; then the club never opens, or the opening is delayed many months. Research the company thoroughly before signing a ''preopening'' contract.

CAUTION   ◆ Don't get cheated by unscrupulous health club owners. While most club owners are honest, the industry has been plagued by ''fly-by-night'' operators. Check with your local better business bureau or consumer affairs office if you think you are being treated unfairly.

   ◆ Initiation fees and monthly dues are often negotiable. Talk to club members to get an idea of the range of possible financial arrangements. Often, initiation fees are transferable; ask about people who might want to sell their membership. The local newspaper is usually a good source for this information.

   ◆ Try the club for a few months before signing a long-term contract. Health clubs make their money from people who do not use the facilities. It will be worth it to try a club on a temporary basis instead of paying monthly dues for years and never going to the facility.

◆ Join a club you can afford. Many clubs charge you a "prestige" fee. If you are a poor college student, it will probably be a waste of your resources to join the "Rockefeller Health Club" for $150 a month. A more modest and less expensive club may provide you with the equipment and activities you need. Shop around!

◆ Don't be pressured into signing a contract on your first visit. Go home and think about the offer. Return only after all your questions have been answered and you are sure the deal is right for you.

◆ Make sure that the contract extends your membership if you have a prolonged illness or go on vacation.

2. The club should be convenient.

◆ You will probably not use the club very often if it is in an inconvenient location.

◆ Beware of memberships that offer reduced dues if you train during "non-prime-time hours." If you only have time to train at 6 A.M., then a discounted early morning membership may be advantageous. But if you want to train immediately after work or school at 5 P.M., then pay the extra money for an unrestricted membership.

◆ Check out the club at the times you plan to train to make sure that you will have easy access to the equipment and exercise classes.

3. The club should have a well-trained staff.

◆ Many universities have degree programs in exercise physiology that call for extensive study in chemistry, physiology, anatomy, nutrition, sports injuries, kinesiology (study of movement), mathematics, and psychology. The best health clubs have staff members with this training. National groups, such as the American College of Sports Medicine, certify exercise leaders after they have shown adequate training and knowledge. It is no longer acceptable for health clubs to rely on poorly trained ex-athletes or ex-body builders for their exercise leaders. Don't join a club with a poorly trained staff!

◆ The club should consider your medical history before putting you on a program. This is especially important if you are over thirty-five years old or have any health problems.

◆ Beware of clubs that do exercise tolerance tests without adequate medical supervision. Organizations such as the American Heart Association and American College of Sports Medicine have strict guidelines regarding exercise stress tests. They call for the presence of a physician if you are over thirty-five or have significant health problems. Some clubs try to get around these regulations by doing submaximal tests. But if your fitness is low, it is very easy for such a test to stress you maximally. Don't let clubs cut corners with your health.

◆ Choose a club that puts its members on systematic programs. Many different weight training programs will improve strength and fitness if practiced systematically. The club should have some way of monitoring your program. Some modern health clubs are so sophisticated that a central computer keeps tabs on your workout as you move from one machine to the next. The next time you work out the computer remembers what you did the time before. For most people, it is unnecessary to be that sophisticated, but some effort must be made to chart your progress.

◆ The club should have established medical emergency procedures.

4. The club should offer amenities besides weight training.

◆ If you have children, does the club offer reliable and reasonable child care? Some clubs offer fitness activities for children.

◆ Is there an opportunity to develop other types of fitness besides strength and power? Well-equipped clubs have other facilities, such as swimming pools; stationary bikes; rowing and stair machines; racquetball, basketball, and tennis courts; and aerobics classes.

◆ Are you socially compatible with the membership? Different clubs attract different types of people. If you tend to be down to earth, you may be better off avoiding a posh, "pretentious" type of health club. Some clubs cater to hard-core body builders, who can sometimes seem very overbearing to the more casual weight trainer. The best way to determine the social environment is to observe the club on several occasions and talk to the members. Find a club where you will fit in.

◆ Many clubs have a juice bar and a shop that sells exercise accessories, such as exercise clothing and weight belts. Although the products may be overpriced, the shops are convenient and could be an important selling point for the club.

WHAT TO WEAR

Women can choose from an exciting variety of exercise clothes. Comfortable and fashionable leotards won't get in the way and look great. Shorts made of elastic material, such as Spandex, hug the body, supplying support. Or, if you prefer, you can wear running shorts and a T-shirt. Almost any standard exercise clothing will do.

Breast Support

While breast support is not as important in weight training as in running or volleyball, it is a good idea to wear a good sports bra whenever you exercise. The breasts are made mostly of fat and are mainly supported by skin and connective tissue. They can be injured from barbells pressing too hard against them or from excessive movement while running on gym treadmills. If you combine weight training with aerobics, then the need for a good bra becomes obvious.

A good sports bra should contain little elastic material, freely absorb moisture, and be easily laundered. It should support the breasts in all directions. Seams, hooks, and catches should not irritate the skin. You might consider buying a bra with an underwire for added support and a pocket to insert padding if you do exercises that could possibly cause injury.

Shoes

Wear shoes that provide good lateral support, such as tennis shoes, aerobics shoes, or cross-training shoes. It is important that you wear shoes at all times, to protect your feet against falling weights and people stepping on them.

If you are interested in competitive weight lifting, consider buying a pair of weight lifting shoes. They provide excellent lateral support and raise your heels slightly so you have better balance during your lifts. These shoes are available through weight lifting magazines or from leading sports shoe manufacturers, such as Adidas, Nike, and Puma. Hiking boots, which provide similar support, are a good substitute.

Weight Lifting Belt

A **weight lifting belt** is worn by the serious weight trainer for back protection. Although the effectiveness of weight lifting belts has not been studied scientifically, many experts think that they support the abdominal muscles, which helps maintain proper spinal alignment when handling heavy weights. While a belt may help during any exercise, it is particularly important when doing squats and pulling exercises.

CAUTION   ◆   Don't rely solely on a belt to protect your back. Good lifting technique and strong, flexible muscles are critical for preventing back injury.

You used to be able to get a weight lifting belt in any color or style — as long as it was brown cowhide! Now belts are made in a variety of colors to complement exercise clothing and look fashionable and attractive. You can buy them through exercise equipment stores or women's fitness magazines.

Wraps

Many advanced women weight trainers use **wraps** to support their knees, wrists, or elbows. Wraps support injured joints and provide extra support. They can be made of elastic bandages, leather, or neoprene. They are unnecessary for the recreational weight trainer.

Some women use wraps to counteract knee pain during and after weight training sessions. While there are many causes of knee pain, it is often caused by the kneecap putting too much pressure on the bone underneath. Knee wraps may actually increase this pressure and make the pain worse. One solution is to buy a knee wrap that has a hole for the kneecap. The hole provides support while reducing pressure on the kneecap.

"Grip wraps" are strips of cotton webbing (such as the webbing used in karate belts) wrapped around the wrist and the weight bar; they take stress from the forearm muscles during lifts such as cleans and lat pulls. The grip is often the limiting factor in these lifts. Grip wraps allow you to use more weight during workouts, so you can make faster progress.

If you become overdependent on grip wraps, grip strength will fail to keep pace with strength in major muscle groups. This may impede your progress. Doing exercises that stress your hands, such as cleans and lat pulls, is one of the best ways to improve grip strength.

Gloves

Weight training can chafe your hands if you don't protect them. Barbells, dumbbells, and some weight machines are knurled (contain small ridges) for better gripping, but the knurls are abrasive. Gloves may prevent you from getting chafed and calloused hands. Buy gloves that fig snugly but follow the contours of the hands, so they don't lose sensitivity. It's probably also a good idea to use hand lotion after a weight workout.

THE STRUCTURE OF THE WEIGHT TRAINING PROGRAM

The structure of your weight training program depends on your goals. Serious body builders may train four to six hours per day, five to six days per week, while fitness "addicts" incorporate weight training into programs involving other activities—such as aerobics, running, cycling, yoga, and swimming. Most people do not have that much time to devote to fitness training, and a minimum commitment of less than a few hours a week will suit some women perfectly.

Weight Machines versus Free Weights

The weight room has gone "high tech." It is amazing to go to a commercial fitness show and see the incredible array of computerized exercise machines that are available: rowing machines that let you compete against a computerized rower; machines that "remember" your last workout and automatically provide the right resistance for you. Are these shiny technological marvels going to make you twice as strong, in half the time, with less work than traditional free weights? No.

Muscles get stronger if you make them work against resistance. You can increase strength by pushing against free weights (dumbbells and barbells), your own body weight, or sophisticated exercise machines. What are the advantages and disadvantages of each? Table 5–1 summarizes the pros and cons of free weights and weight machines.

Exercise machines are most women's preferred method of weight training because they are safe and convenient. All that is needed is to set the resistance (usually done by

---

TABLE 5–1
A Comparison of Free Weights and Exercise Machines

EXERCISE MACHINES

Advantages	*Disadvantages*
• Safe	• Expensive to buy
• Convenient	• Expensive to maintain
• Don't require spotters	• Inappropriate for performing dynamic movements
• Provide variable resistance	• Only offer limited number of exercises
• Have high-tech appeal	
• Require less skill	
• Make it easy to move from one exercise to the next	

FREE WEIGHTS

Advantages	*Disadvantages*
• Allow dynamic movements	• Not as safe
• Develop control of weight	• Require spotters
• Help overcome strength differences between the two sides of the body	• Require more skill
• Allow greater variety of exercises	• Can cause equipment clutter
• Cheaper to buy	• Cause more blisters and calluses
• Cheaper to maintain	

---

placing a pin in the weight stack), sit down on the machine, and start exercising. You don't have to bother anyone for a spot (assistance) or worry about a weight crashing down on you.

Also, free weights tend to twist in your hands when you try to balance them, which can cause blisters and calluses, whereas using weight machines requires little or no balancing. So, beginners find the machines easier to use.

Weight machines also provide different amounts of resistance as you do the exercise — the weight is heavier as the exercise progresses. The theory behind this feature is that the stress on the muscle is more uniform as it contracts through its range of motion. It is not known whether this feature is superior to the resistance supplied by free weights.

Lastly, weight machines are appealing to many people because they appear to be technologically advanced.

Few skilled strength-speed athletes train on machines. Their programs center on three main exercises: presses (bench press, incline press, etc.), pulls (cleans, snatches, etc.), and squats. Explosive lifts, such as the pulls, are difficult or impossible to mimic exactly on machines. Machines restrict you to a few movements, while many exercises are possible with free weights.

Popular weight machines are expensive to buy and expensive to maintain. An elementary free-weight set can be purchased at a fraction of the cost. However, to equip a gym with a full array of free-weight equipment, including Olympic weights, dumbbells, and racks, is also very expensive. So the choice between weight machines and free weights shouldn't be based on cost alone.

Many coaches and athletes believe that free-weight exercises are essential for developing explosive strength for sports. Because free weights are not on a controlled track the way machine weights are, you must control them, which probably helps to increase strength. Free weights help to overcome asymmetrical strength and let you do a greater variety of exercises.

So which is better? Unless you're training seriously for a sport calling for a great deal of strength, training on machines is probably safer, more convenient, and just as effective as training with free weights. Free weights demand balance and greater muscle coordination; they tend to provide more complete development of strength in a particular movement. You can increase strength either way, so it really boils down to personal preference.

Number of Training Sessions Per Week

Most women should train between two and four days per week. Two days per week is the minimum necessary to improve strength. But after the early phases of training, two days per week tends to only maintain strength, rather than improve it. Training fewer than two days per week leads to muscle soreness and injury and is not recommended.

Training too much is also a bad idea. Excessive training often leads to overtraining and delayed progress. Studies show that heavy training days invariably lead to tissue damage. Damaged tissue needs time to recover before the next intense session. Also, more training is not necessarily better training. Training intensity is the primary factor determining increased strength. A person who trains too often and too hard never recovers enough to train intensely. Sometimes it is better to rest than to train.

CAUTION ◆ Training too many days per week can lead to overtraining and injury. The body needs time to adapt. Sometimes, it is better to train less often but more intensely.

Four-day-a-week programs are popular with some athletes during peak seasons dedicated to conditioning. Typically, they will work the upper body two days per week and the lower body the other two days. For example, Monday and Thursday would be devoted to training the upper body, and Tuesday and Friday to the lower body.

For most women, a three-day-a-week schedule is optimal.

Warm-up

Most experts agree that **warm-up** is essential before exercise, and empirical evidence suggests that warm-up improves performance and prevents injury. Warm-up raises body

---

TABLE 5–2
Benefits of Warm-up

- Increased muscle temperature (faster chemical reactions in muscles)
- Increased tissue elasticity
- Increased tissue blood flow
- Increased joint lubrication
- Pre-exercise practice

---

temperature so that the muscles respond better. It increases tissue elasticity, making it less prone to injury, and promotes joint lubrication. Also, intense exercise without warm-up may place the heart at risk. (See Table 5–2.)

CAUTION   ◆   Always warm up before exercise. Adequate warm-up may enhance performance and prevent injury.

Warm-up can be either general or specific. General warm-up involves the whole body — large-muscle exercises such as jumping jacks, stretching, running in place, or stationary cycling. Specific warm-up involves doing the same lift you intend to begin your program with, but using a lighter weight. For example, a woman who plans to do 3 sets of 10 repetitions of 80-pound bench presses might do 1 set of 10 repetitions with 20 pounds as a warm-up. Similar warm-up exercises would be done for each major lift that forms the program.

Cool-down

Cool-down returns muscle temperature and metabolic rate to normal levels. Cool-down after weight training usually consists of relaxing. In contrast, after endurance exercise it is important to gradually wind down the tempo of activity. Because weight training is not a continuous activity, winding down is unnecessary — unless you drastically increase your heart rate during the workout. In that case, it is a good idea to do an active cool-down during recovery, such as riding a stationary bicycle at a slow cadence and no friction on the fly-wheel.

Stretching after a workout is recommended by many experts. Postexercise stretching may help prevent muscle soreness. Also, it is a particularly good time to work on flexibility because the muscles and joints are warmed up.

Don't shower or take a whirlpool bath immediately after a vigorous weight training workout. This is critical. During intense training, blood is shunted to the skin and muscles, and hormones are mobilized to help you do heightened physical activity. Taking a hot shower immediately after exercise places stress on the heart that may not be tolerated by some people. Give yourself at least five to ten minutes to relax first.

CAUTION   ◆   Cool down after a workout before taking a hot shower or whirlpool bath. Exercise causes blood to be shunted to the skin for cooling and to the muscles for exercise metabolism. The combination of inadequate cool-down and exposure to a hot shower or whirlpool after exercise could result in fainting or other problems.

Choosing the Correct Starting Weight

Don't use too much weight when you begin your program. It is always better to err on the side of safety. For the first set, choose a weight that you can move easily for at least 10 repetitions. (Again, a repetition is one execution of the exercise, and a set is a group of repetitions followed by a rest.) If you aren't sure about a good starting weight, use only the barbell or the lowest weight on the exercise machine. You can always add weight later.

Do only one set of each exercise during the first workout. The exercises may feel very easy to do, but you must be careful not to overexert yourself or you will get excessively sore. Recent studies suggest that delayed muscle soreness (soreness experienced one to two days after a workout) is caused by tissue damage. Some delayed muscle soreness is very common, and perhaps necessary for improved strength, but excessive soreness suggests that you trained too hard.

The first weeks of weight training should be devoted to learning the exercises. Not only do you have to understand how to do the exercises, but your nervous system has to learn to communicate with the muscles so that you can exert the necessary force. This takes time. Gradually add sets to your program. By the end of the second week of training, you should be doing a complete workout.

During later training sessions, gradually add weight until you are bearing a significant load and the 10-repetition set becomes difficult. The time to add weight is when you can finish each set with relative ease. If you feel as though you can do 11 or 12 repetitions with a particular weight, it's time to add more resistance. If after adding weight you can do only 8–9 repetitions, stay with that weight until you can again complete the 10 repetitions per set. But, if after adding weight you can do only 4–6 repetitions, then you have added too much weight, and some must be removed.

Experienced weight trainers should avoid using too much weight after a layoff. Muscle soreness and injury will result if you try to resume where you left off. As described in chapter 3, getting in shape gradually is a basic principle of training. Excessive training loads do not encourage the body to adapt faster; they only cause injury and delay progress.

CAUTION   ◆   Don't use too much weight after coming off a layoff because you may get sore or injured.

Sets and Repetitions

The ideal number of sets and repetitions is determined by your goals. Generally, if you want increased endurance, do more repetitions (10 or more) and more sets (3 or more). If your primary goal is increased strength, do fewer repetitions and use more weight.

TABLE 5-3 Example of a Beginning Weight Training Program		
EXERCISE	SETS	REPETITIONS
Bench press	3	10
Lat pull	3	10
Lateral raise	3	10
Biceps curl	3	10
Triceps extension	3	10
Abdominal curl	3	10
Leg press	3	10
Calf raise	3	10

Doing 4–6 repetitions per set for 3–5 sets is best for developing strength. Women who are interested in doing single maximum lifts must occasionally do 1–3 repetition sets, so they can adjust to the heavier weights. Experienced weight trainers use a variety of combinations of sets and repetitions. (Some of these will be discussed in the following section on cycling techniques.)

Beginners should start off with more repetitions and lighter weights. This gives the tissues a chance to adjust gradually to increased loading, minimizing the chances of injury. After the first two weeks, it is best to do 3 sets of 10 repetitions of 6–8 exercises. Practice this program, gradually increasing the weight, for at least two months before decreasing the number of repetitions in each set. If you are not interested in increasing strength rapidly, you may never want to do fewer than 10 repetitions per set. An example of a modest beginning weight training program appears in Table 5–3. These exercises can be done with free weights or weight machines.

Several training systems use a technique called **pyramiding**, which contains built-in warm-up. In pyramiding, an exercise is practiced for 3 or more sets, increasing the weight during each set. This technique was originally introduced by T. L. DeLorme in the 1950s. DeLorme recommended 3 sets of 10 repetitions for each exercise with weight progressively increasing from 50 percent to 75 and 100 percent of maximum capacity.

There are many other systems for regulating loads, including the **constant set method, failure method, circuit training, super sets**, and **giant sets** (Table 5–4). Some of these techniques reduce the weight during later sets after reaching the maximum weight. Any technique you choose should allow you to warm up before you significantly load your muscles.

Basic Cycling Techniques

Many women go to the gym three to five days a week and "kill" themselves doing the same lifts each time with as much weight as they can handle. Hard work is a cornerstone of

---

TABLE 5–4
Selected Weight-Set-Repetition Methods

CIRCUIT TRAINING

Uses 6–20 exercise stations set up in a circuit (i.e., in series). The person progresses from one station to the next, either performing a given number of repetitions or doing as many repetitions as possible during a given time period (for example, 20 seconds) at each station.

CONSTANT SET METHOD

The same weight and number of sets and repetitions are used for each exercise. Example: Bench press 5 sets of 5 repetitions at 80 lbs.

PYRAMID METHOD

Uses multiple progressive sets, either ascending or ascending-descending, for each exercise. Variations: increasing weight while decreasing repetitions, or decreasing weight while increasing repetitions.

Ascending pyramid

Set 1	5 repetitions	75 lbs.
Set 2	5 repetitions	100 lbs.
Set 3	5 repetitions	120 lbs.

Ascending-descending pyramid

Set 1	5 repetitions	75 lbs.
Set 2	5 repetitions	100 lbs.
Set 3	5 repetitions	120 lbs.
Set 4	5 repetitions	100 lbs.
Set 5	5 repetitions	75 lbs.

---

progress in any program, but unless it is applied correctly, it is worthless. Training is properly directed if it makes the body adapt as rapidly as possible to improve its function or its appearance. But misdirected hard work results in overtraining and is counterproductive.

Many elite athletes use a powerful technique called cycle training, or periodization of training. This technique allows the body to adapt rapidly without overtraining and prepares it to accept and benefit from intense workouts.

In cycle training, the type, volume, and intensity of training is varied throughout the year. In athletics, for example, the year is often divided into off-season, preseason, early season, and peak season. The weight training program is different during each part of the year.

During the off-season, the athlete does general conditioning exercises. The program is designed to keep her in shape but also provide mental and physical rest from the rigors of

---

TABLE 5–4
Selected Weight-Set-Repetition Methods — *continued*

DeLORME METHOD

3 sets of 10 repetitions at 50, 75, and 100 percent of maximum. Example for a person who can do 10 repetitions at 100 lbs:

Set 1	10 repetitions	50 lbs. (50%)
Set 2	10 repetitions	75 lbs. (75%)
Set 3	10 repetitions	100 lbs. (100%)

SUPER SETS

Usually uses two exercises, typically with opposing muscle groups, in rapid succession.

Set 1	10 repetitions	30 lbs.	knee extensions
Set 1	10 repetitions	15 lbs.	knee flexion
Rest			
Set 2	10 repetitions	30 lbs.	knee extension
Set 2	10 repetitions	15 lbs.	knee flexion
Rest			
Repeat			

GIANT SETS

Uses multiple exercises in succession for the same muscle group.

Set 1	10 repetitions	75 lbs.	Bench press
Set 1	10 repetitions	5 lbs.	Dumbbell fly
Rest			
Set 1	10 repetitions	75 lbs.	Bench press
Set 1	10 repetitions	5 lbs.	Dumbbell fly
Rest			
Repeat			

---

training. A tennis or field hockey player might run, play volleyball, swim, and do some circuit training. She would also do some light training in her sport to maintain her skill.

During the preseason and early season (sometimes called the "load phase"), if the goal is to develop maximum power for a strength-speed sport, such as track and field, the program is devoted to developing base fitness. The weight training program would involve much volume (5 sets of 5–8 repetitions for the major exercises, at moderately high intensities). This phase is typically very exhausting.

The peak phase (competitive phase) is devoted to achieving peak performance. The weight training program involves high-intensity workouts with much less volume than the preseason and early-season phases. The athlete is given plenty of rest between intense workouts, a technique that allows her to "peak," that is, to achieve her best performance. If workouts and rest are timed correctly, top performances can be predicted.

Each major cycle contains microcycles in which the volume, intensity, and rest vary from workout to workout or from week to week. The purpose of these microcycles is to allow muscle systems adequate recovery time. According to several studies, intensity is the chief factor in enhancing fitness. In traditional training programs, athletes train hard every session, which may lead to overtraining. Microcycles prepare people for intense training days by giving them time to recover.

In this way, cycle training encourages the body to adapt systematically with a minimum risk of injury. Small gains are made over a long time, and peak performance happens at a predetermined time in the season. Part of the basis for this method is that individuals adapt better to changing stimuli than to a constant program—partly because learning is fastest when a new activity is introduced and partly because change is psychologically stimulating.

Considerable muscle and connective tissue damage happens during and after intense endurance or strength training. While the relationship between the rate of healing and the structure of the training program is not known, common sense tells us there is such a relationship. Muscle fibers probably need to heal to some extent before they can be safely stressed again.

Cycle techniques are ideal for women doing general conditioning programs. It is unnecessary to do the same exercises every session using the same weights. Vary your program. Do some exercises intensely during one workout and other exercises intensely during the next. A basic three-days-per-week conditioning program using the cycle training technique is shown in Table 5–5.

Making Progress

Initially, gains seem to come easily, but every woman will reach a plateau where little progress is made. Because the body adapts rapidly at first, many gains are due as much to learning new exercises as to actual changes in the muscles. The best thing to do when you're not improving anymore is to examine your program. The cause is usually too much work, not enough work, or a bad program.

If you're working very hard every session, never miss a workout, and are still not making any progress, then maybe you're doing too much. Try cycling your workouts, or take a week or two off. Rest can do amazing things—often you can expect to return to personal records in the weight room if you just take a brief rest.

But sometimes you may not work hard enough. Are you only going through the motions when you train, not putting much effort into the exercises? Try adding more weight for at least one set of each exercise, even if it makes you do fewer repetitions. Make sure you complete each workout—if you have a habit of cutting a few exercises out of the program each session, that can amount to a lot of work not accomplished after a few weeks.

Many people get enough rest, complete their workouts, but still do not make progress. Then the answer is to change your program. The body adapts quickly to exercises at first but slows after the first month or so. You can often begin to make progress again by changing your program. Do exercises slightly different from the ones you usually do. For example, if you do bench presses on a machine or with barbells, try switching to the incline press. Changing the way you do a lift sometimes helps you make progress. Sometimes

TABLE 5–5
An Example of Cycle Training for General Conditioning

MONDAY

Exercise	Sets	Repetitions	Weight (lbs.)
Bench press	4	10	60
Lat pulls	3	10	30
Squats	4	10	80
Abdominal curls	3	20	—
Back extensions	3	15	—
Arm curls	3	10	25
Triceps extensions	3	10	15

WEDNESDAY

Exercise	Sets	Repetitions	Weight (lbs.)
Incline press	3	10	40
Modified pull-ups	5	5	—
Pull-overs	3	10	20
Leg presses	3	10	150 (machine)
Calf raises	4	20	150 (machine)
Abdominal curls	3	40	—
Good mornings	3	10	15

FRIDAY

Exercise	Sets	Repetitions	Weight (lbs.)
Bench press	3	10	50
Lat pulls	3	10	40
Squats	3	10	70
Abdominal curls	3	20	—
Back extensions	3	15	—
Arm curls	4	10	30
Triceps extensions	4	10	20

Note: Exercises can be done on weight machines or with free weights. Notice that exercises and the amount of weight used in an exercise vary from one workout to the next. Exercises are described in chapters 6–10.

having a spotter help you so that you can use more weight will help get you over the hump. If you are doing normal grip bench presses, change your grip; do the exercise with a narrower or wider grip.

Another effective technique is to add exercises that strengthen muscles needed for the primary exercises. For example, doing bar dips is effective in improving the bench press. If

---

TABLE 5–6
Safety Rules for Weight Training

Weight training can be dangerous if safety guidelines are not followed. The following are basic principles for preventing injuries in the weight room.

- Lift weights from a stabilized body position.
- Be aware of what is going on around you.
- Stay away from other people when they are busy doing exercises. Bumping into them could result in injury.
- Always use collars on barbells and dumbbells.
- Remain clear of the weight stack when someone else is using a weight machine.
- Don't use defective equipment. Report malfunctions immediately.
- Protect your back by maintaining control of your spine (protect your spine from dangerous positions). Observe proper lifting techniques and use a weight lifting belt for heavy lifts.
- Don't hold your breath. Avoid the Valsalva maneuver (trying to expire while holding your breath). This results in greatly reduced blood flow from the heart and could cause fainting.
- Always warm up before training.
- Don't exercise if you're ill.

---

you have trouble doing dips, have a spotter put his or her hands around your waist and help you with the movement. Knee extensions will improve the squat. Change the exercise, and your body will again adapt more quickly.

COMBINING WEIGHT TRAINING WITH OTHER SPORTS AND EXERCISES

Intense weight training can be exhausting, thus interfering with performance in other activities. After a vigorous weight training session, you may be more susceptible to injury if you immediately do another sport. If possible, get plenty of rest after an intense workout before participating in a sport where you might get injured. If most of your program consists of general conditioning exercises, schedule strength and endurance workouts on different days. At least schedule intense weight training on light endurance training days. If you go to an aerobics class on the same days you weight train, go to the class first.

TABLE 5–7
Skills and Responsibilities of the Spotter

- Be strong enough to assist with the weight being lifted.
- Know the proper form of the exercise and the spot.
- Know the number of repetitions being attempted.
- Establish signals for beginning and ending the exercise with the lifter.
- Pay constant attention during the lift, but don't interfere unless necessary or requested.
- Pay particular attention to collars or weight plates that are sliding and if the weight trainer is using asymmetrical lifting techniques (i.e., moving one arm at a different speed than the other). These situations may require immediate intervention.

PREVENTING ACCIDENTS

Accidents and injuries do happen in weight training. Maximum physical effort, elaborate machinery, rapid movements, and heavy weights can combine to make the weight room a dangerous place if you don't take proper precautions. The basic principles of preventing accidents in the weight room are presented in Table 5–6.

Spotting

Spotters help the lifter move the weight into position to begin a lift, actively help with the lift, and help during an unsuccessful repetition (see Table 5–7). Helping with the weight after a failed repetition is the most critical responsibility of the spotter, who must be quick to go to the lifter's aid if necessary. Usually, you will need one or two spotters. However, during a bench press or incline press, one spotter is sometimes preferable because it is easier to coordinate between one spotter and a lifter than between two spotters and a lifter. During a squat, you will need two spotters, one to stand on either side of the weight and help if the lift cannot be finished.

CAUTION   ◆   Use spotters whenever you might be in danger of missing a lift and being caught under the fallen weight.

The lifter must indicate when the weight is to be removed. If the spotter intervenes and removes the weight too soon, the lifter may be deprived of making her best effort to complete the lift. But if there is too much delay in removing the weight, the lifter may suffer an injury. Spotters must position themselves so as to be ready to help the lifter if needed, and they must observe proper lifting techniques themselves: bend the knees, maintain a straight back, and keep the weight close to the body (Figure 5–1). During the lift, spotters should be attentive but should not disrupt the lifter's concentration.

CAUTION ◆ Spotters must be wary of injuring themselves. Use proper lifting techniques when spotting someone.

When you use spotters to help move a weight into position to begin an exercise, coordination between the spotters and the lifter is again important. Signals should be worked out before, so that everyone understands when the weight is to be raised from the rack. For example, the lifter may count "one, two, three" with the weight being lifted into position on "three." It's best to work with the same spotters regularly because you'll learn what to expect from each other after a while.

You will sometimes want a spotter to actively help with the exercise, using either free weights or weight machines. When doing negative exercises (eccentrics), the spotter may do most of the work for you during the active phase of the lift. The spotter can also provide just the extra amount of force needed to finish an exercise. Lifters sometimes call this help the "magic fingers," because the spotter may be able to help complete a lift by lifting with just a couple of fingers.

Figure 5–1 Proper technique for spotting

Collars

A **collar** is a device used to secure a weight to a barbell or dumbbell. It is quite common to see people lifting weights without collars, but to do so is dangerous. In weight training, it is easy to lose your balance or to raise one side of the barbell faster than the other. If this happens and you're not using collars, the weights on one side of the bar can easily slip off, resulting in the weights on the opposite side crashing to the floor. Obviously this can knock you off balance and lead to injury.

CAUTION   ◆   Always be sure to use collars, and be sure that they secure properly.

Preventing Accidents on Weight Machines

One of the attractions of weight machines is their safety. But weight machines are not totally harmless, so you should be cautious around them. Keep away from moving weight stacks. It's very easy to get hurt if someone jumps on the machine ahead of you and begins an exercise while your fingers are close to the weight stack. Be particularly attentive when changing weights.

When doing exercises, stay away from moving parts and weight plates. Also, don't walk near a machine when someone else is on it — you may break her concentration or bump into her while she's doing an exercise.

Many weight machines can be adjusted to accommodate people of different sizes. Make sure the machine is properly adjusted and locked in place before you begin an exercise — it could be dangerous to begin an exercise only to have the machine move suddenly.

Beware of broken machines. Broken bolts, frayed cables, broken chains, and loose cushions can give way and cause serious injury. If you notice a machine is broken or close to it, tell an instructor immediately.

Make sure the machines are clean. Equipment upholstery should be cleaned daily. Dirty vinyl is a breeding ground for germs that can cause skin diseases. A good practice is to carry a towel around with you and place it on the machine where you sit or lie down. That way you won't have to bathe in someone else's sweat.

Behavior in the Weight Room

Weight trainers should always have the utmost respect for the equipment because misuse can lead to a serious injury. Fooling around in the weight room can cause injury. Be attentive to what's happening around you.

Medical Considerations

While weight training is safe, accidents do happen. Report any obvious injury to muscles or joints to the instructor or a physician. Don't keep working out in the hope that the pain will go away. Training with an injured joint or muscle usually leads to more serious injury.

Be careful not to overdo. It's easy to strain or cramp a muscle by doing one too many sets of repetitions. If you do injure yourself, either work on another body part or take the rest of the day off. Make sure you get the necessary first aid. Even minor injuries heal faster if you use the ''RICE'' principle: Rest, Ice, Compression, Elevation.

Weight training tends to increase blood pressure, which in some people can cause serious medical problems. In people with heart disease, weight training can cause various symptoms, such as arm or chest pain. Consult a physician if you are having any unusual symptoms during exercise or if you are not sure that weight training is a proper activity for you.

CAUTION ◆ Report any headaches; chest, neck, or arm pains; dizziness; labored breathing; numbness; or visual disturbances to the instructor immediately.

PROPER MECHANICS OF EXERCISE

Each exercise has a proper technique. These techniques will be discussed in chapters 6–10. Several principles, however, are common to all exercises. These principles will help you prevent injury and derive the maximum benefit from your weight training program.

Lifting Techniques

Back injuries are among the most serious that can happen in the weight room. They can be prevented if you follow some basic principles of lifting.

◆ Keep the weight as close to your body as possible. The farther out you hold a weight, the more strain on your back.

◆ Do most of your lifting with your legs. The large muscles of the thighs and buttocks are much stronger than those of the back, which are better suited to maintaining an erect posture. Keep your hips and buttocks tucked in.

◆ When picking up a weight from the ground, keep your back straight and your head level or up. Bending at the waist with straight legs places tremendous strain on the muscles and spinal disks of the lower back.

◆ Don't twist your body while lifting. Twisting places an uneven load on back muscles, causing strain.

◆ Lift the weight smoothly, not with a jerking, rapid motion. Sudden movements place more stress on the spinal muscles and disks.

◆ Allow for adequate rest between lifts. Fatigue is a prime cause of back strain.

- Lift within your capacity. Don't lift beyond the limits of your strength.
- If training on a weight machine, make sure that it is properly adjusted to your body. Uncomfortable, twisted positions may place unnecessary stress on vulnerable spinal muscles and nerves.

Breathing

Never hold your breath when you lift. Exhale when exerting the greatest force, and inhale when moving the weight into position for the active phase of the lift. Holding your breath while straining to perform a lift (called ''Valsalva's maneuver'') causes a decrease in blood returning to the heart, which means that blood cannot be pumped as easily to the brain. It can make you dizzy and faint.

Exercise Movements

Exercises should be done smoothly and in good form. With practice, you will ''groove'' your lift, so that the weight is moved in the same general way every time you do the exercise.

Generally, move the weight into position for the active phase of the exercise slowly and with control. Lift or push the weight forcefully during the active phase of the lift. Obviously, if you are using enough resistance, these powered movements have to be slow — but you should still try to do the movements explosively. An old weight lifting saying to remember is to ''go down slow and up fast.''

You should not ''bounce'' the weight against your body during the exercise. Bouncing means that you make an explosive transition between the pushing and recovery phase of the lift. Advanced weight trainers sometimes do this so they can practice an exercise using heavier weight. This practice is not recommended, however, because it can cause serious injury.

CAUTION   ◆   Never bounce a weight against the body.

Do all lifts through the full range of motion. Limiting the range of motion will increase strength only in the part of the range you are exercising. Practiced correctly, weight training improves flexibility. ''Muscle-boundness'' — the inflexibility developed from weight training — happens only when exercises aren't done through a full range of motion.

Grips

Use the correct grip for each lift. There are three basic types of grip: **pronated** (palms away from you), **supinated** (palms toward you), and **dead-lift** (one palm toward you, one away). The pronated grip is used in most presses, pulls, and squats. The supinated grip is used in exercises such as biceps curls and chin-ups. The dead-lift grip is used in the dead-lift exercise to increase your grip strength. (See Figure 5–2.)

Figure 5–2 Basic barbell grips: (a) pronated grip, (b) supinated grip, (c) dead-lift grip

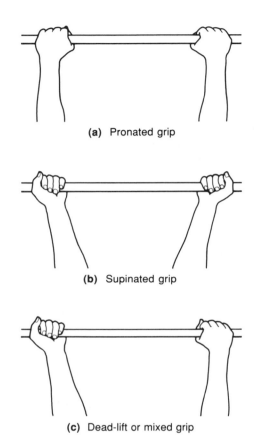

(a) Pronated grip

(b) Supinated grip

(c) Dead-lift or mixed grip

The thumbless grip and thumblock grip are not recommended. The thumbless grip, as the name implies, involves placing the thumb in the same plane as the fingers. Although this grip places the thumb under less stress, it is dangerous. For example, in a bench press you could easily lose control of the weight, and it could fall on you. The thumblock grip, in which the thumb is wedged between the index and middle fingers, places the thumb at increased risk of injury.

C H A P T E R

6 Developing the Chest and Shoulders

THE CHEST AND SHOULDERS ARE MORE DIFFICULT TO DEVELOP IN WOMEN THAN MEN BE-
cause women carry less muscle mass in that area of the body. However, many sports require
a strong upper body. Strong chest and shoulder muscles are an advantage when serving a
tennis ball, for example, or rock climbing, or wind surfing. Chest and shoulder exercises
will build the strength and power you need to excel in these and other activities.

There is no exercise, however, that will increase the size of the breasts—although
fortunes have been made on exercise devices that promised breast development. Breast
tissue is largely made of fat. If the size of the chest muscles is increased, the breasts may
look a little larger. But since women have a limited ability to increase muscle size through
weight training, don't expect miracles from doing a few bench presses.

The major muscles of the chest and shoulders are **multipennate**, which means that
the muscle fibers are aligned in several directions. Because of this, you need to do several
different exercises to fully develop these muscles. For example, the pectoralis major (the
principle muscle of the chest) can be divided into upper, middle, and lower parts according
to how the muscle fibers are aligned. To completely train and develop this muscle, you must
do exercises that build each of the muscle's three segments. Likewise, the deltoid (the
principle muscle of the shoulder) is a three-part muscle that requires three or more exercises
to develop it fully.

It is extremely difficult to present exercises that functionally isolate specific muscle
groups. For example, exercises for the chest, such as the bench press, also train the muscles
of the arm, back, abdomen, and, to a limited extent, the legs (the legs stabilize the upper
body in some chest and shoulder exercises). Throughout chapters 6–10, exercises are
grouped according to the body part they work the best.

Also, it would be difficult and cumbersome to list exercises for each of the many types of weight machines on the market. Therefore, we present exercises that can be done using free weights and on Universal Gyms and Nautilus machines. We are not endorsing these machines. We're using them because they are the most common machines found in gyms in the United States and Canada and are popular with many women. There are many fine weight machines made by other manufacturers that will build strength as well. When using other machines, follow the basic guidelines for the machine exercises described in the text. They will usually be appropriate.

EXERCISES TO BUILD THE CHEST

The pectoralis major is the principle muscle of the chest. It is used in bringing the arm across the chest and lowering the arms when they are overhead. It is also very important in any movement that involves pushing. It is used for the forehand in tennis, to throw a ball, and in free-style swimming.

The principal exercises to develop the chest include:

◆ Bench press (barbell, dumbbell, power rack; chest press, Universal)

◆ Incline press (barbell, dumbbell; modified using incline bench and Universal shoulder press)

◆ Fly (dumbbell; forty-degree chest/shoulder, ten-degree chest, and arm cross machines, Nautilus)

◆ Pullover (barbell; pullover machine, Nautilus)

◆ Decline press (barbell, dumbbell; decline press machine, Nautilus; modified chest press, Universal)

Bench Press

The bench press is probably the most popular weight training exercise. It provides strength and power that can be carried over to many sports and develops well-shaped muscles that look good. This exercise primarily develops the chest, the front of the shoulders, and the back of the arms.

◆   THE TECHNIQUE   Lying on a bench on your back with your feet on the floor, grasp the bar at shoulder width with your palms upward, away from your body (Figure 6–1). Lower the bar to your chest, and then return it to the starting position. The bar should follow an elliptical path, during which the weight moves from a low point at the chest to a high point over the eyes. Inhale when lowering the bar, and exhale when pushing it.

CAUTION   ◆   During the motion, be careful not to arch your neck or back; this could result in injury to the spinal disks. Never bounce the weight off your chest because this could injure the ribs, sternum (breast bone), or internal organs.

Figure 6–1 (a, b) Bench press, (c) narrow-grip bench press places more stress on the triceps muscles

Muscles developed: pectoralis major, deltoid, triceps brachius

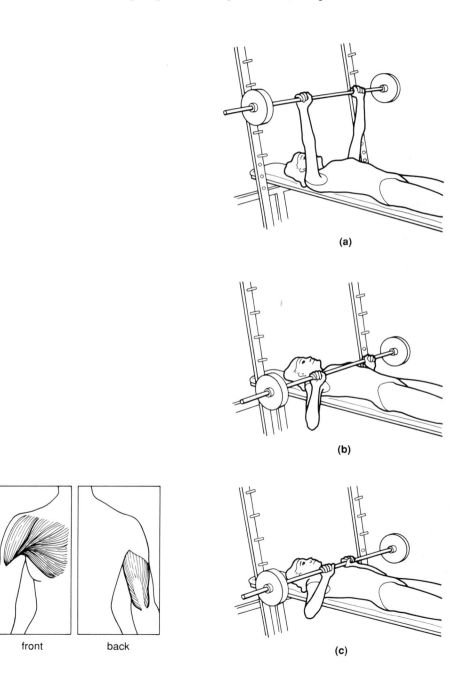

(a)

(b)

front   back

(c)

It is best to use a bench with a built-in **rack**. The rack should be constructed so that the weight can be taken on and off with little danger of pinching your hands. The rack and bench should be sturdy enough so that large weights can be supported safely. The bench should allow your arms and shoulders to travel freely during the exercise.

You can try emphasizing different muscle groups by varying the width of your grip. To increase the stress on the back of your upper arms (triceps muscle), narrow your grip; to stress the chest more, use a wider grip.

Chest Press, Universal Gym

◆   THE TECHNIQUE   Lying on a bench on your back with your feet on the floor and head toward the machine, grasp the handles at shoulder width with your palms upward (Figure 6–2). With the chest press machine, the starting point of the exercise is with the handles at chest level. Push the handles upward until your arms are fully extended. Return to the starting position without banging the weights together. Exhale when pushing the weight, and inhale when lowering it.

Universal recommends that you compensate for a stronger right or left arm by moving the hand of your weaker arm farther out on the handle, about half again as far out as the other hand.

It is difficult to predict from performance on the Universal chest press machine how much weight you could lift with free weights. The chest press incorporates a device that progressively increases the resistance as you do the exercise. Thus, the weight is heavier at the end of the movement than at the beginning.

CAUTION   ◆   Be careful not to put your head too close to the weight stack when lying on the bench. Make sure the weight pin is fully inserted.

Variations of the Bench Press

Variations of this lift will help increase your bench press capacity or are good alternatives to it. Two variations are the dumbbell bench press and power rack bench press.

◆   THE TECHNIQUE   Dumbbell bench press (Figure 6–3): You will only be able to handle a fraction of the weight in this exercise, as compared to the barbell bench press. To perform the dumbbell bench press, begin by sitting on the bench with dumbbells resting on your knees. Carefully rock backward until your back is on the bench and the dumbbells are in your hands and resting on your chest. Push the dumbbells overhead until your elbows are extended, then return the dumbbells to your chest.

◆   THE TECHNIQUE   Power rack bench press (Figure 6–4): This exercise is used to overcome sticking points you may experience during the bench press. The power rack allows you to place pegs, or stops, at various points within the vertical range of motion.

Figure 6–2 Universal chest press

Muscles developed: pectoralis major, deltoid, triceps brachius

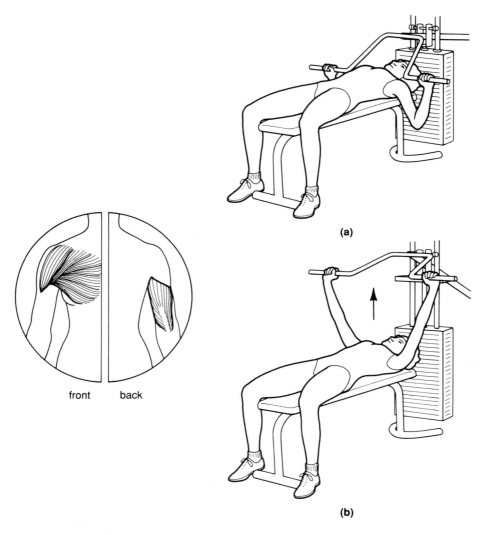

(a)

front   back

(b)

Place a bench inside the power rack, and select three positions along the range of motion used during the exercise. The first pegs should be placed so that the bar can rest close to your chest. Lying in the basic bench-press position with the bar resting on the first pegs, push the weight overhead. After you have completed your workout at the first pegs, move the pegs so that the bar rests in the middle of the range of motion. Repeat the exercise sequence. Finally, move the pegs so that the bar travels only a few inches during the exercise. At this level, you will be capable of handling much more weight than you can normally bench press. It's a safe way to get used to increased weight.

Figure 6–3 Dumbbell bench press

Muscles developed: pectoralis major, deltoid, triceps brachius

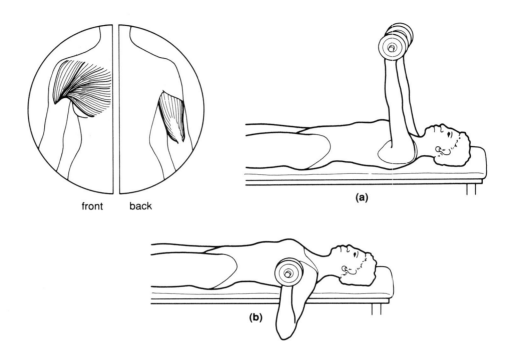

front   back

(a)

(b)

Figure 6–4 Power rack bench press

Muscles developed: pectoralis major, deltoid, triceps brachius

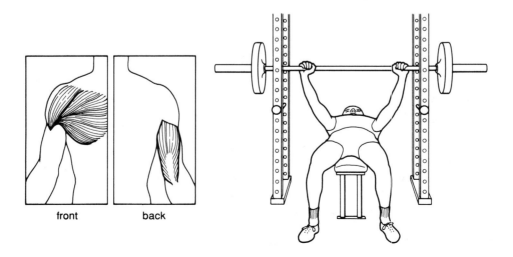

front   back

A number of auxiliary exercises can be included in the training program to help improve your bench press. Incline presses, flys, and parallel bar dips will be described in the following sections.

Incline Press

The incline press is similar to the bench press except that the path of the bar is at a forty-five-degree angle to the plane of the chest, rather than perpendicular to it. The exercise is performed while standing or sitting on a slant board. It develops the upper chest, the front of the shoulders, and the back of the arms and tends to give the chest a rounder appearance. You can simulate the incline press on the Universal gym by placing an incline bench within the shoulder press machine.

◆   THE TECHNIQUE   Lying on an incline bench, grasp the bar at shoulder width and lower it to the upper part of your chest (Figure 6–5). Push the bar upward until your arms are extended. While pushing the weight, remember that it is important to direct the bar upward toward the top of the head. Lower the weight to the starting position. Don't lower

Figure 6–5 Incline bench press

Muscles developed: upper pectoralis major, deltoid, triceps brachius

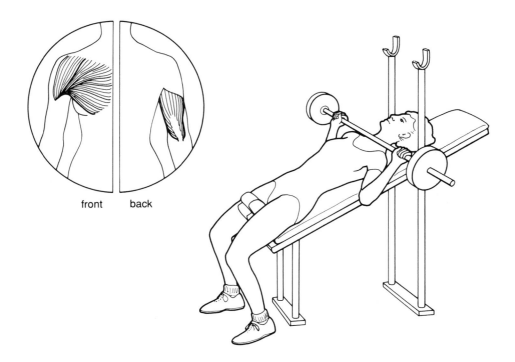

front   back

the bar farther down your chest. You will need spotters on this lift to handle maximum loads. A rack will also help you use heavier weight and will make spotting safer and easier.

CAUTION ◆ Pushing the weight too far in front of you will make the exercise more difficult to perform and may result in a back, shoulder, or elbow injury.

The incline press may be executed with a barbell or with dumbbells. Special skill is required to lift dumbbells to the starting position of the exercise. While sitting or standing on the incline bench (depending upon which type of bench you are using), grasp the dumbbells and place them on your knees. Beginning with the dumbbell in your left hand (if you are right-handed), vigorously flex your knee upward, pushing the dumbbell into the starting position. Repeat this procedure with your other arm. After you have completed the exercise, slowly lower the dumbbells, either one at a time or both together, back to the floor.

Modified Incline Press, Universal Gym

◆ THE TECHNIQUE   Place an incline bench (the long, straight type) between the handles of the shoulder press station of the Universal gym (Figure 6–6). The bench should be aligned so that when you lie on it, your back is to the machine. Push the handles upward until your arms are extended, then lower the weight without banging the plates together.

Dumbbell Flys

Flys develop the chest and the front part of shoulders. They are done with dumbbells or machines that simulate the use of dumbbells. Universal and Nautilus make machines that simulate this movement. This is a good exercise for developing the appearance of fullness of the chest.

◆ THE TECHNIQUE   Lie on a flat-bench (a bench without racks) with a dumbbell in each hand, palms facing inward, and arms extended straight above your chest (Figure 6–7). Slowly lower the weights to the side until they reach shoulder level, then return to the starting position. As you get stronger, lower the weight below shoulder level. Do this exercise with the arms bent slightly. Straight-arm flys should be avoided because of danger to the elbows. Flys can also be done on an incline or decline bench. Incline flys tend to work the upper part of the chest, while decline flys work the lower part of the chest.

CAUTION ◆ Don't use too much weight when you first start doing dumbbell flys because there is a possibility of injuring your elbows. Also, don't do straight-arm flys for the same reason.

Figure 6–6 Universal incline press

Muscles developed: upper pectoralis major, deltoid, triceps

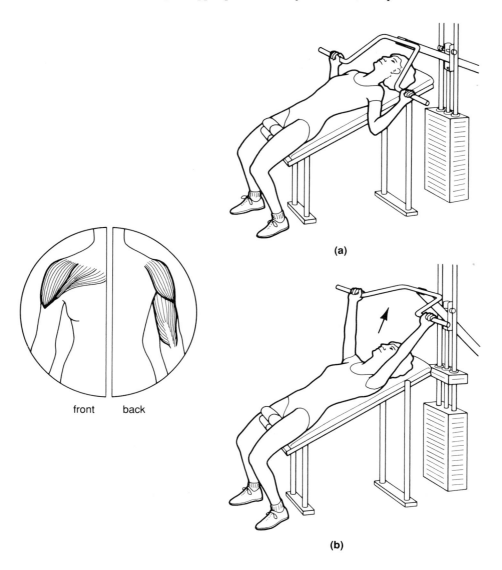

(a)

front   back

(b)

"Fly" Machines, Nautilus

Nautilus and several other equipment manufacturers make machines that simulate dumb-bell flys. They may be superior to using free weights because they allow you to better isolate the chest and shoulder muscles.

Figure 6–7 Dumbbell flys: (a) bent arms, (b) straight arms

Muscles developed: pectoralis major, anterior deltoid

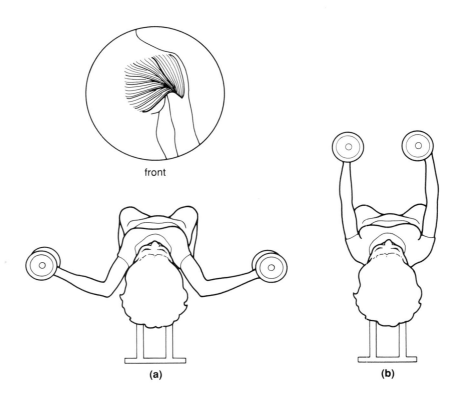

(a)   (b)

◆   THE TECHNIQUE   The arm cross is part of the Nautilus double chest machine (which also includes the decline press). Align the bench so that your upper arms are perpendicular to your torso (Figure 6–8). You should sit back as far in the seat as you can so that you are exercising from a supported position. Grasp the handles so that your forearms are resting against the pads. You should feel a slight pull in your chest muscles in this starting position. Pushing with your forearms (not your hands), bring the elbows as close as you can in front of your chest. Universal, as well as several other manufacturers, make similar exercise machines.

Forty-Degree Chest/Shoulder and Ten-Degree Chest Machines, Nautilus

◆   THE TECHNIQUE   These machines are similar in many ways to the arm cross machine, except the incline benches are at different angles and they use large cylindrical pads rather than handles to move the weight (Figure 6–9). On each of these machines,

Figure 6–8 Nautilus arm cross

Muscles developed: anterior deltoid, pectoralis major

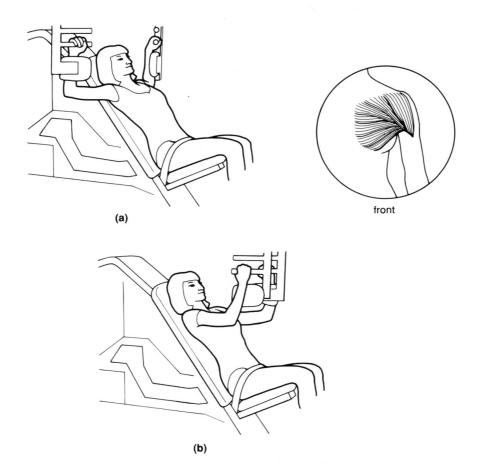

(a)

front

(b)

adjust the seat so that the tops of your shoulders are lined up with the cams (the movement points) of the machines. Lying on the bench on your back, with your arms under the pads (pads should be placed at the bottom of your biceps muscles), move the pads together until they are over the center of your chest. Try to use your chest muscles as much as possible to do the movement.

Pullovers

Pullovers are good for developing the pectoralis major (large chest muscle), rib muscles, and lats (i.e., latissimus dorsi, a large muscle of the back). This exercise can be done with either free weights or machines.

Figure 6–9 Nautilus forty-degree chest/shoulder, ten-degree chest machines

Muscles developed: pectoralis major, anterior deltoid

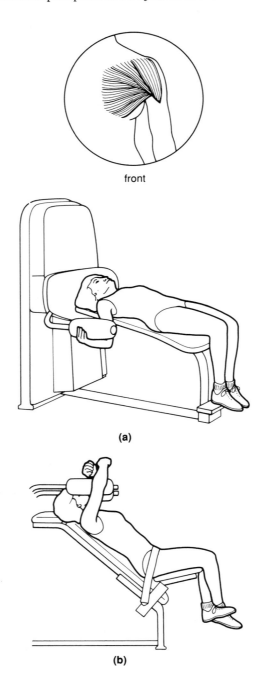

front

(a)

(b)

Figure 6–10 (a, b) Barbell bent-arm pullovers, (c, d) straight-arm pullover

Muscles developed: latissimus dorsi (back), pectoralis major (front)

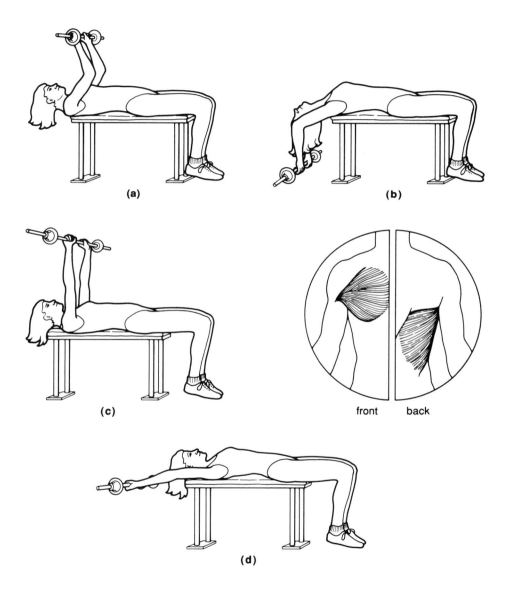

(a)

(b)

(c)

front   back

(d)

◆   THE TECHNIQUE   Lie on your back on a bench; your head should extend slightly beyond the end of the bench (Figure 6–10). Grasp a barbell with hands about eight inches apart. With arms bent slightly, lower the bar behind your head and reach toward the floor. Return to the starting position. As a variation to bent-arm pullovers, you can work with straight arms, but then less weight should be used to prevent elbow injury.

Figure 6–11 Universal Gym bent-arm pullovers

Muscles developed: latissimus dorsi, pectoralis major

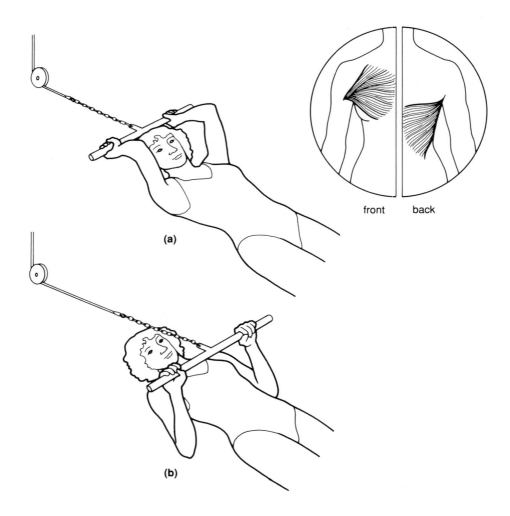

front   back

(a)

(b)

You can also do these exercises on the low pulley station of Universal Gym (Figure 6–11). The exercises are identical to those described for free weights, except that they are done on the floor.

A single dumbbell can be used in place of the barbell. Usually this variation is performed with the bench placed perpendicular to the weight trainer (Figure 6–12).

Pullover Machine, Nautilus

◆   THE TECHNIQUE   Adjust the seat so that your shoulders are aligned with the cams (Figure 6–13). Push down on the foot pads with your feet so that you can place your elbows

Figure 6–12 Dumbbell pullovers

Muscles developed: pectoralis major (front), latissimus dorsi (back)

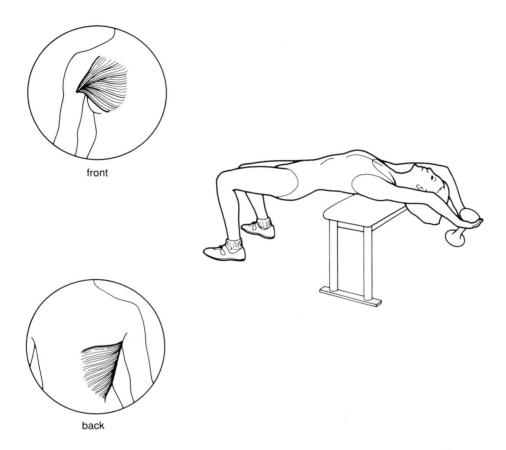

front

back

on the pads. Rest your hands lightly on the bar. To get into the starting position, let your arms go backward as far as possible. Then pull your elbows forward until the bar almost touches your abdomen.

Decline Bench Press

The decline bench press is not usually part of the typical weight training routine. Body builders use it to develop the lower part of the pectoralis major muscle. It also builds the front part of the shoulders and the backs of the arms.

Doing decline presses with free weights requires a specialized piece of equipment called a "decline bench." A decline bench can be made by placing blocks under one end of a flat bench. Using this technique, you can do decline bench presses on the Universal Gym. When using free weights, make sure the bench is steady and use spotters during this exercise. If you fail to complete this exercise, the weight could fall on your neck or face.

Figure 6–13 Nautilus pullover machine

Muscles developed: pectoralis major (front), latissimus dorsi (back)

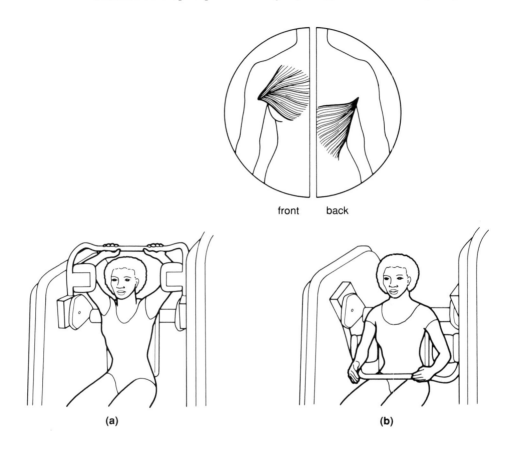

front   back

(a)   (b)

◆   THE TECHNIQUE   Lie on a decline bench, face up, with head downward (Figure 6–14). Grasp the weight at shoulder width, bring it to your chest, and then press it upward until elbows are extended. This exercise can also be done using dumbbells.

Decline Press, Nautilus Double Chest Machine

A decline bench press exercise station is part of the Nautilus double chest machine.

◆   THE TECHNIQUE   Adjust the seat so that the tops of the handles are aligned at the tops of your armpits (Figure 6–15). Grasp the handles with palms toward you. Push the levers until your arms are fully extended.

Figure 6–14 Decline press

Muscles developed: lower pectoralis major, deltoid

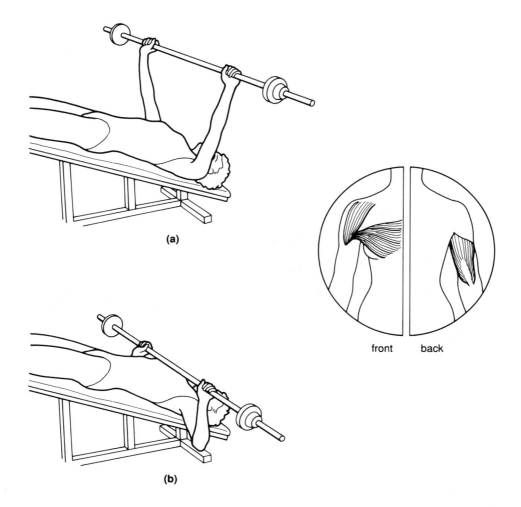

(a)

(b)

front   back

Other Exercises to Develop the Chest

Many other exercises develop the chest muscles to some extent, including lat pulls, catching and throwing medicine balls, and working with "crushers" (specialized exercise devices that use movements resembling dumbbell flys). Horizontal push presses — in a standing position, pushing a weight horizontally as rapidly as possible — also develop the chest. And that old stand-by, push-ups, is a good chest exercise that doesn't require any equipment.

Figure 6–15 Nautilus decline press

Muscles developed: pectoralis major, deltoid, triceps

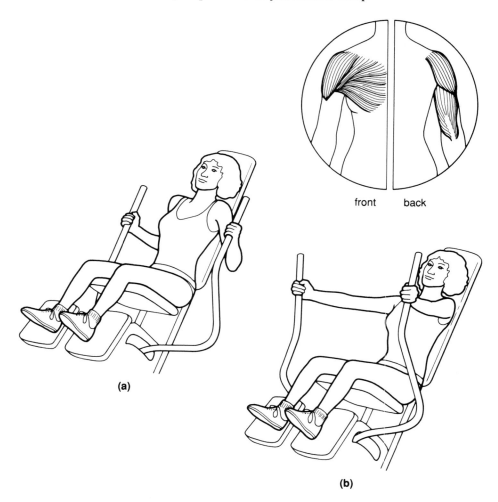

front   back

(a)

(b)

EXERCISES TO DEVELOP THE SHOULDERS

The shoulder is one of the most complex joints of the body, composed of six joints and more than twelve different muscles. The rest of this chapter focuses on the principal exercises that develop the shoulder's major muscle groups. Also, exercises to train the "rotator cuff" muscles will be described. The rotator cuff group, comprising four deep shoulder muscles, is important because it is often injured by swimmers and by volleyball, softball, and tennis players.

While all the exercises described in the previous section ("Exercises to Build the

Chest") train the shoulder muscles as well, the following exercises are generally recognized as the best for developing the major muscles of the shoulder:

◆ Overhead press (shoulder press)
◆ Behind-the-neck press
◆ Raises
◆ Upright rowing

Overhead Press

The overhead press, also known as the "military press," can be done standing, seated, and with barbells or dumbbells. Universal and Nautilus, as well as numerous other manufacturers, make shoulder press machines.

CAUTION ◆   When standing, be careful not to arch the back excessively, or you may injure the spinal muscles, vertebrae (bones of the spine), or disks.

You should use a belt when doing unsupported overhead lifts, such as overhead presses. This exercise develops the deltoids (the large triangular muscles that cover the shoulder joints), the upper chest, and the back of the arms.

◆   THE TECHNIQUE   The overhead press with a barbell begins with the weight at your chest, preferably on racks (Figures 6–16 and 6–17). If you are a more advanced weight trainer, you can "clean" the weight to your chest. The clean should be attempted only after instruction from a knowledgeable coach.

1. The clean: To perform the clean, place the bar on the floor in front of you. Keep your feet approximately one to two feet apart. Grasp the bar, palms down, with your hands at slightly more than shoulder width, and squat down, keeping your arms straight, your back at a thirty-degree angle, and your head up. Pull the weight up past your knees to your chest while throwing your hips forward and shoulders back. Much of the power for the clean should come from your hips and legs.
    Ask your weight training instructor or coach to teach you this lift because doing it improperly can lead to injury. If you are not an experienced weight trainer, use a rack to place the weights in the starting position.

CAUTION ◆   Do not attempt the clean unless you have some weight training experience and receive proper instruction from a knowledgeable coach.

2. The overhead press: Push the weight overhead until your arms are extended, then return to the starting position (weight at chest). Again, be careful not to arch your back excessively.

Figure 6–16 The clean is often used to move the bar into the starting position for the overhead press

Muscles developed: deltoid (front and back), triceps (back), trapezius (back)

Figure 6–17 Standing press

Muscles developed: deltoid (front and back), triceps (back), trapezius (back)

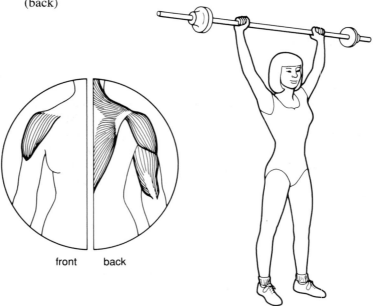

front   back

Figure 6–18 Nautilus overhead press machine

Muscles developed: deltoid, triceps, trapezius

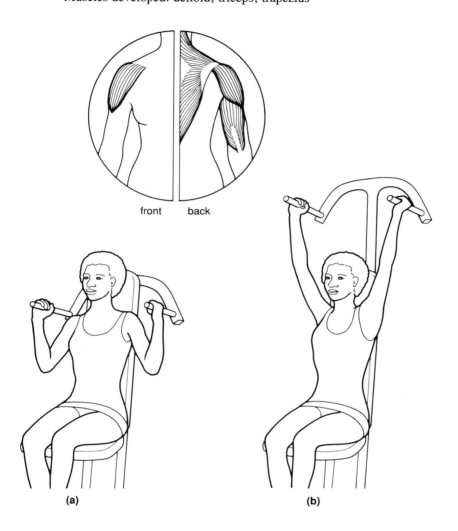

front   back

(a)   (b)

Overhead Press Machine, Nautilus

◆   THE TECHNIQUE   Adjust the seat so that the two bars are slightly above your shoulders (Figure 6–18). Sit down, facing away from the machine, and grasp the bars with palms facing inward. Press the weight upward until your arms are extended.

Figure 6–19 Universal overhead press machine

Muscles developed: deltoid, triceps, trapezius

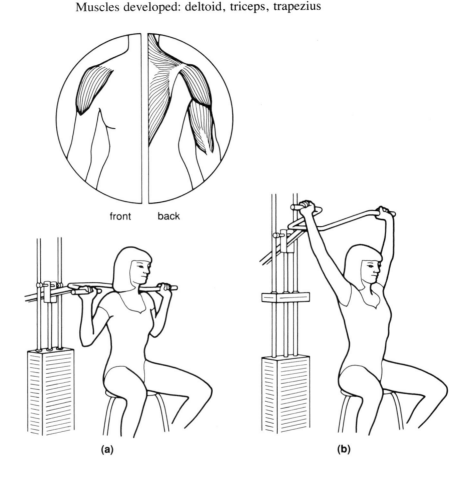

Overhead Press Machine, Universal Gym

◆   THE TECHNIQUE   Place a high stool next to the overhead press station so that when you sit down and face the machine, your shoulders almost touch the handles (Figure 6–19). Grasping the handles with hands facing the machine, push the bar overhead until your arms are extended. Don't arch your back or lean forward excessively. Try to do this exercise with your shoulders.

Behind-the-Neck Press

A variation of the standing press is the behind-the-neck press. This exercise develops the shoulders, back of the arms, and upper back muscles. Avoid this exercise if you have a

Figure 6–20 Behind-the-neck press

Muscles developed: deltoid, triceps, trapezius

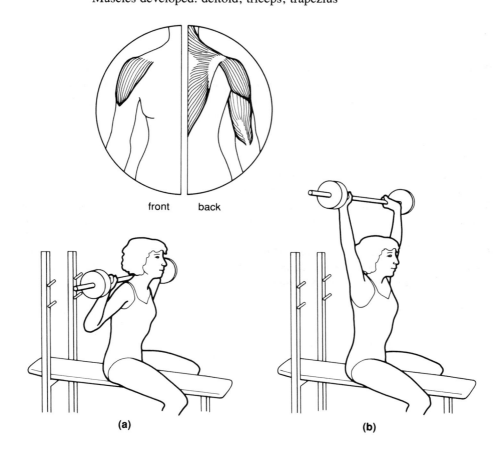

front   back

(a)   (b)

rotator cuff injury because it can pinch sensitive tissues in the upper shoulder and make the condition worse.

◆   THE TECHNIQUE   This exercise can be done standing or seated and requires a barbell. Use a rack to place the weight in the starting position (Figure 6–20). With a fairly wide grip, place the weight behind your head and rest it on your shoulders. Push the weight above your head until your elbows are extended and then return to the starting position.

Behind-the-Neck Press, Universal Gym

◆   THE TECHNIQUE   This exercise is done exactly the same way as the overhead press on the Universal Gym except that you face away from the machine instead of toward it. Start with the bar even or slightly in front of your shoulders to avoid strain on the rotator cuff muscles.

Raises

Raises are used to develop the deltoid muscle, a three-part, round muscle making up the most prominent part of the shoulder. This exercise must be done to the front, side, and rear to fully develop the deltoid. Raises are usually done with dumbbells, although they can be done with wall pulleys or on specialized exercise machines (see Nautilus lateral raise exercise below).

◆   THE TECHNIQUE   Lateral raises (Figure 6–21): From a standing position, with a dumbbell in each hand and arms straight, lift the weights on both sides until they reach shoulder level, then return to starting position. Bend your arms slightly if your elbows hurt. Some people continue the exercise until the weights meet overhead, but this is inadvisable as it may injure your shoulders. Lateral raises develop the middle section of the deltoid muscle.

◆   THE TECHNIQUE   Front raises (Figure 6–22): In a standing position, using dumbbells or a barbell, and with arms straight, lift the bar in front of you to shoulder level, then return to starting position. This exercise develops the front part of the deltoid muscle.

◆   THE TECHNIQUE   Rear (bent-over) lateral raises (Figure 6–23): This exercise requires dumbbells. In a standing or seated position, with knees bent slightly, bend at the waist. Lift the weights to the side until they reach shoulder level; return to starting position. Bent-over lateral raises develop the back portion of the deltoids.

Figure 6–21 Lateral raises

Muscles developed: deltoid

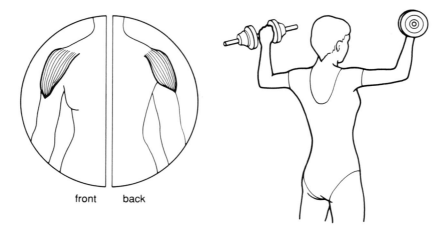

front   back

Figure 6–22 Front raises

Muscles developed: anterior deltoid

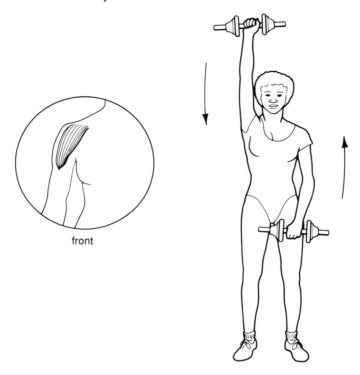

front

Figure 6–23 Bent-over lateral raises

Muscles developed: posterior deltoid, trapezius

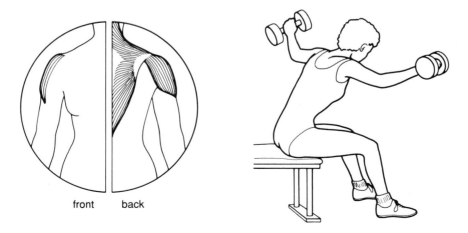

front   back

Figure 6–24 Nautilus lateral raise machine

Muscles developed: deltoid

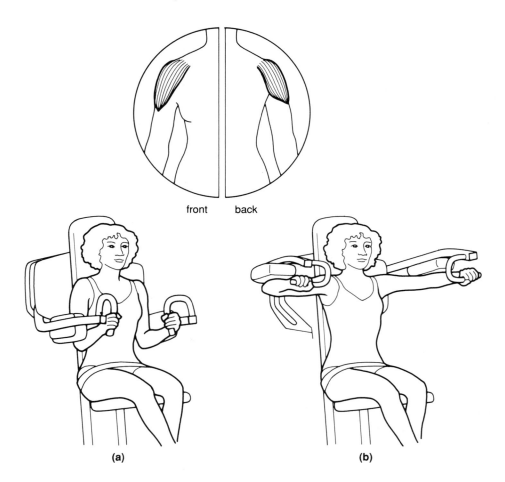

front   back

(a)   (b)

Lateral Raise Machine, Nautilus

◆ THE TECHNIQUE   Adjust the seat so that pads rest just above your elbows when your arms are at your sides and your hands are forward (Figure 6–24). Lightly grasp the handles and push the pads to shoulder level with your arms. Return to the starting position. Lead the movement with your elbows rather than trying to lift the bars with your hands.

Seventy-Degree Shoulder Machine, Nautilus

◆ THE TECHNIQUE   Set the seat so that the cams are even with your shoulders (Figure 6–25). Place your arms under the pads so that they rest just below your biceps on the

Figure 6–25 Nautilus seventy-degree shoulder machine

Muscles developed: deltoid, pectoralis major

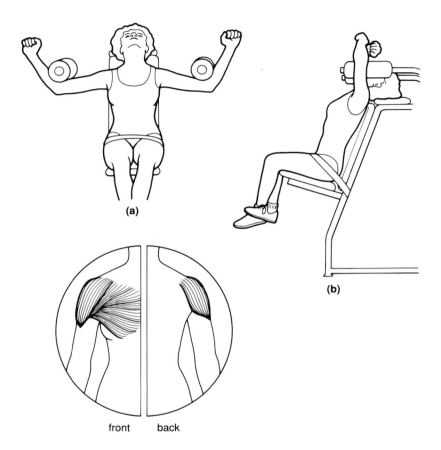

inside of the elbow joint. Move both arms toward the middle of your chest until the two pads almost touch. Return to the starting position.

Upright Rowing

Upright rowing develops the shoulders, the front of the arms, the neck, and the upper back. Because it affects so many large muscle groups at the same time, it is an excellent upper body exercise.

◆   THE TECHNIQUE   Using a pronated grip, grasp a barbell with hands close together and stand with the weight at waist level (Figure 6–26). Pull the weight to the upper part of your chest, then return to the starting position.

Figure 6–26 Upright rowing

Muscles developed: deltoid (front), trapezius (back), rhomboid (back)

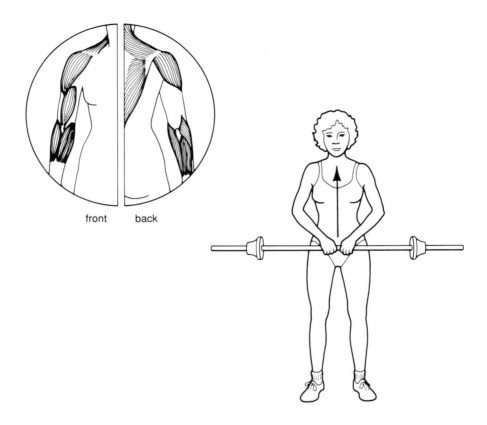

front   back

Upright Rowing, Universal Gym

◆   THE TECHNIQUE   Upright rowing on the Universal Gym uses the same basic technique as with free weights. Adjust the chain of the low pulley station so that the weights you're using go above the weight stack when you stand with the bar at your abdomen (Figure 6–27). Stand far enough away so that the cable does not touch the weight stack.

Rotator Cuff Exercises

The rotator cuff of the shoulder is composed of four muscles that cause the humerus (the large bone of the upper arm) to rotate (turn) inward and outward. This muscle group is often injured in activities that require the arm to go above shoulder level, such as swimming,

Figure 6–27 Universal upright rowing machine

Muscles developed: deltoid, trapezius, rhomboid

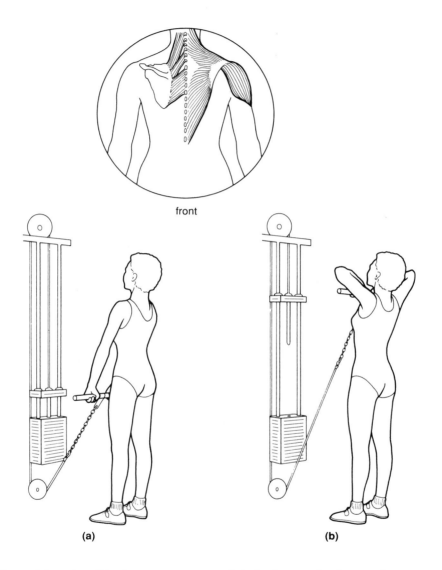

front

(a)   (b)

tennis, and throwing. The best way to prevent injuries is to make the muscles strong and flexible. Three exercises to strengthen this muscle group include:

◆ Dumbbell internal rotation
◆ Dumbbell external rotation
◆ Empty can exercise

Dumbbell External Rotation

This exercise strengthens the muscles that cause the arm to rotate outward (infraspinatus and teres minor).

◆   THE TECHNIQUE   Lie on your side on a table, resting on one elbow (Figure 6–28). Bend your other elbow halfway (ninety degrees), keeping the elbow tight to the rib cage. Slowly lower the weight, and then lift it back to the starting position.

Figure 6–28 Exercise to strengthen the external rotator muscles of the shoulder

Muscles developed: infraspinatus, teres minor

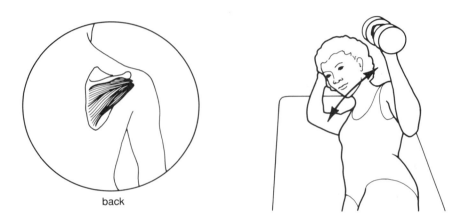

back

Figure 6–29 Exercise to strengthen the internal rotator muscles of the shoulder

Muscles developed: subscapularis

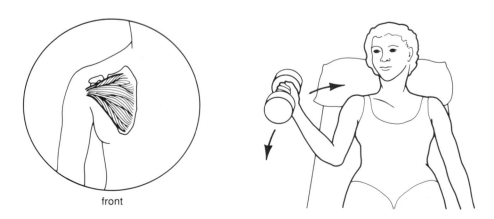

front

Dumbbell Internal Rotation

This exercise develops the muscles that cause the shoulder to rotate inward (subscapularis).

◆   THE TECHNIQUE   Lie on your back on a table with your elbow bent halfway (ninety degrees) and held tightly against your side and with your hand extended over your chest (Figure 6–29). Slowly lower the weight to your side, and then slowly lift it back to the starting position.

Empty Can Exercise

This is probably the most important rotator cuff exercise because it strengthens the supraspinatus muscle, the muscle of the rotator cuff group that is most often injured in sports.

◆   THE TECHNIQUE   Stand upright and hold a dumbbell in each hand (Figure 6–30). Keeping your arms straight, raise your arms to shoulder height, move them horizontally about thirty degrees, and rotate them inwardly as much as possible so that palms are facing the floor. Slowly lower and raise the weights through a forty-five-degree arc. It looks as if you are emptying liquid from two cans — that's how the exercise got its name.

Figure 6–30 Empty can exercise to strengthen the supraspinatus

Muscles developed: supraspinatus, deltoid

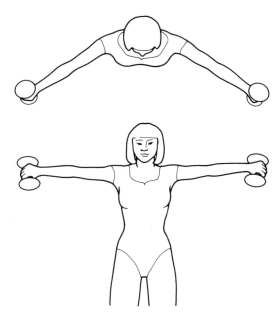

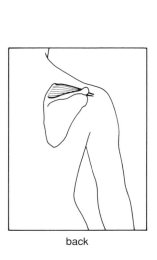

back

CHAPTER

7 Developing the Arms

WE USE OUR ARMS FOR ALMOST EVERY ACTIVITY IN WORK AND PLAY. IT HELPS TO HAVE strong arms for a wide variety of tasks — gardening, opening a can of peanut butter, throwing a ball, playing tennis. Strong and attractive arms are within reach of anyone who will devote a small amount of time to developing them.

This chapter presents basic arm and forearm exercises as well as specialized exercises for preventing "tennis elbow" and increasing grip strength. For the sake of this discussion, the exercises are divided into three categories: the front of the arm, the back of the arm, and the forearm.

EXERCISES FOR THE FRONT OF THE ARM

Curls are the best exercises for developing the muscles of the front of the arm. The principal muscles of this area are the biceps brachius and the brachialis. Curls can be done using a barbell, dumbbells, special curl bars, or curl machines made by Nautilus, Universal Gym, or other manufacturers. Sometimes you may want to use a curl bar (Figure 7–1); it helps to

Figure 7–1 The curl bar

reduce stress on the forearm muscles, allows you to use more weight, and prevents injury to your forearms.

You can do many variations of curl exercises, including:

◆ Standing barbell curls

◆ Dumbbell curls

◆ Preacher curls

◆ Reverse curls

◆ Curl machine, Nautilus

◆ Double arm curls, low pulley station, Universal Gym

Standing Barbell Curls

This is the old standby for developing biceps strength. Be sure not to bend your back when doing this exercise, or you may hurt yourself. If you use heavy weights, it's a good idea to use a weight lifting belt. If your forearms start getting sore after a few weeks, you are probably straining the muscles. Switch from a straight bar to a curl bar.

◆   THE TECHNIQUE   From a standing position, grasp the bar with your palms upward, your hands shoulder-width apart (Figure 7–2). Keeping the upper body rigid, bend

Figure 7–2 Standing barbell curl

Muscles developed: biceps, brachialis

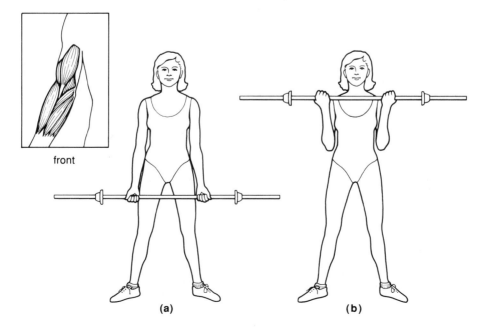

front

(a)   (b)

(flex) your elbows until the bar reaches a level slightly below the collarbone. Return the bar to the starting position.

CAUTION   ◆   To avoid injury, do not arch your back during this exercise. Standing with your back against the wall will help keep your back straight. If you are lifting heavy weights, use a weight lifting belt.

Dumbbell Curls

There are many ways of doing dumbbell curls — seated on a flat bench or seated on an incline bench; alternating between arms, doing both arms at the same time, or doing all the repetitions with one arm before doing them with the other arm. Although there is little difference between these variations, each one stresses the arm in a slightly different way. You can change your routine with these variations to add interest to your program.

◆   THE TECHNIQUE   While seated on a flat or incline bench, grasp the dumbbells with a supinated grip (palms up) (Figure 7–3). Begin with the arms extended, bend the arms until the weights approach your shoulders, and then return to the starting position. Swinging the weights or bending your back while doing dumbbell curls will make the exercise less effective.

Figure 7–3 Seated dumbbell curl

Muscles developed: biceps, brachialis

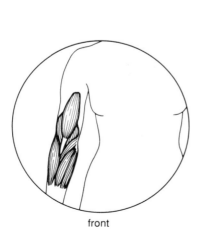

front

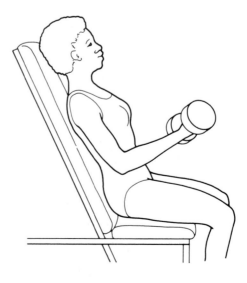

Preacher Curls

The preacher curl is an exercise that effectively isolates the biceps, the muscles of the front of the arm. The reason this lift is so effective is that it is extremely difficult to cheat while doing it. It requires a special apparatus called a "preacher stand," so named because it resembles a pulpit. If a preacher stand is not available, an incline bench can be substituted.

◆   THE TECHNIQUE   This lift can be done using a barbell, dumbbells, or curl bar. Using a supinated grip, place your elbows on the preacher stand and fully extend your elbows. Bend your arms ("curl" the weight) until the bar almost reaches your collarbone, then return to the starting position (Figure 7–4).

Figure 7–4 Preacher curls using preacher stand

Muscles developed: biceps, brachialis

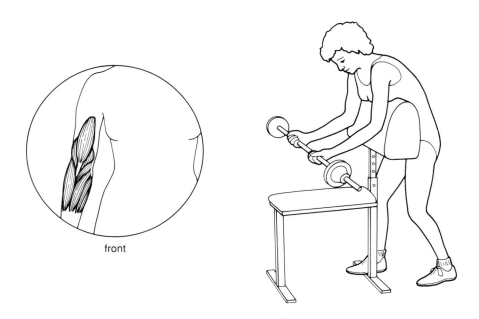

front

Reverse Curls

Reverse curls have an effect similar to the preacher curls, except they place a different stress on the forearm muscles. You can do this exercise with a barbell, dumbbell, or curl bar and in a seated or standing position.

◆   THE TECHNIQUE   Stand holding the weight at your waist, using a pronated grip (palms down, opposite of preacher curls). Lift the weight by bending at your elbows until the bar almost reaches your collarbone, then return to the starting position (Figure 7–5).

Figure 7–5 Reverse curls (note grip)

Muscles developed: biceps, brachialis, brachioradialis

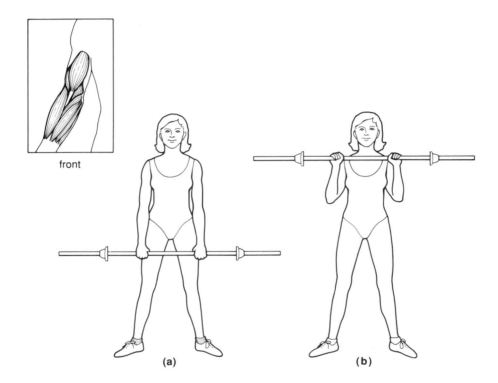

front

(a)   (b)

Curl Machine (Multibiceps), Nautilus

This machine exercise resembles the preacher curl with free weights. It is excellent for isolating the biceps muscle.

◆   THE TECHNIQUE   Adjust the seat so that your upper arms are almost parallel with the supporting pad (Figure 7–6). You should be able to comfortably bend your arms through their full range of motion. Grasp the handles and extend your lower arms (starting position). Flex your arms as much as possible while keeping your elbows on the supporting pad, then return to the starting position.

Figure 7–6 Nautilus curl (multibiceps) machine

Muscles developed: biceps, brachialis

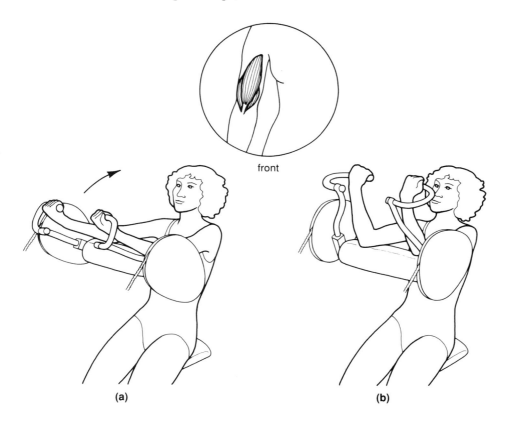

front

(a)   (b)

Double Arm Curl, Low Pulley Station, Universal Gym

The same basic technique is used for curls on the Universal Gym as with free weights.

◆   THE TECHNIQUE   Adjust the chain of the low pulley station so that the weights you're using go above the weight stack when you stand with the bar at your abdomen (Figure 7–7). With hands at waist level, grasp the bar with a supinated grip (starting position). Keeping your elbows close to your sides, curl your elbows until the weight touches your upper chest, then return to the starting position.

Other Exercises for the Front of the Arm

Any exercise that adds stress to the arm muscles as you bend your elbow will work this part of your body. Exercises that work the biceps, as well as other muscle groups, include pull-ups, chin-ups, lat pulls, and rowing exercises.

Figure 7–7 Double arm curls, low pulley station, Universal Gym

Muscles developed: biceps, brachialis

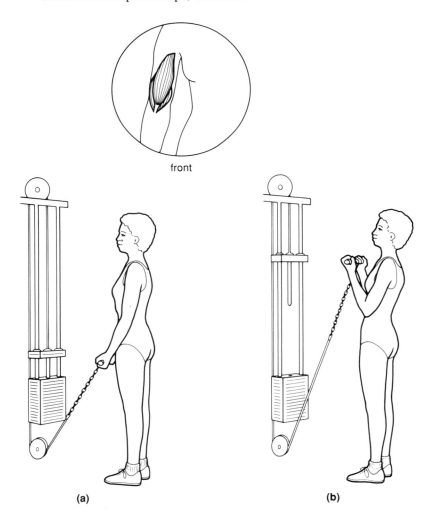

front

(a)   (b)

EXERCISES FOR THE BACK OF THE ARM

The triceps is the major muscle of the back of the arm and is trained during all pressing exercises. Exercises that are particularly good for building the triceps include the following:

- ◆ Triceps extensions on the lat machine
- ◆ French curls

◆ Bench triceps extensions
◆ Parallel bar dips
◆ Triceps extensions, Nautilus multitriceps machine

Triceps Extensions on the Lat Machine

The triceps extension on the lat machine is an excellent exercise for isolating the triceps muscles. This exercise can be done on the Universal Gym or Nautilus lat machine stations or on a free-standing lat machine. If you develop elbow pain as a result of doing this exercise, try another of the triceps exercises listed above.

◆   THE TECHNIQUE   Using a narrow, pronated grip, grasp the bar of the lat machine and fully extend your arms with your elbows held closely at your side (Figure 7–8). From this starting position, with elbows locked to your side, allow your hands to be pulled up to your chest; then firmly push the weight back to the starting position. If your elbows move during this exercise, you are cheating.

Figure 7–8 Triceps pushdowns

Muscles developed: triceps

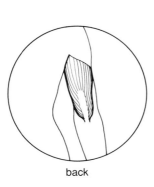

back

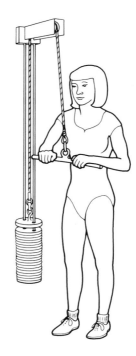

French Curls

This exercise looks similar to the behind-the-neck press, which develops the shoulders (see chapter 6), but done properly, it is very effective in isolating the triceps. The basic difference between the two exercises is that the behind-the-neck press involves movement of both the shoulder and elbow joints, while in French curls the shoulders are fixed and the movement occurs only in the elbows.

◆   THE TECHNIQUE   Grasp a barbell behind your head, using a pronated grip with hands approximately seven to twelve inches apart (Figure 7–9). Keeping your elbows up and stationary, extend your arms until the weight is overhead, then return to the starting position. While somewhat awkward, this exercise can also be done using one handle on the seated press station of the Universal Gym.

Figure 7–9 French curls (seated triceps extensions)

Muscles developed: triceps

back

(a)   (b)

Bench Triceps Extension

This exercise is similar in many ways to French curls.

CAUTION   ◆   Be careful not to use too much weight, because if you lose control of the bar during this exercise, you could seriously injure yourself.

◆   THE TECHNIQUE   Lie on a bench, grasping a barbell with a pronated grip, hands seven to twelve inches apart (Figure 7–10). Push the weight above your chest until your arms are extended (this is the starting position). Keeping your elbows in a fixed position, carefully lower the weight until it touches your forehead, then push the weight back to the starting position.

Figure 7–10 Bench triceps extension

Muscles developed: triceps

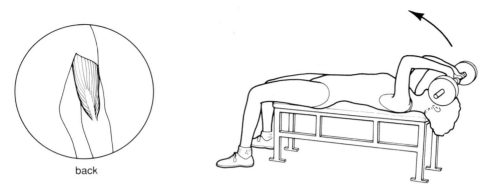

back

Figure 7–11 Parallel bar dips

Muscles developed: triceps, trapezius, deltoid, latissimus dorsi, pectoralis major

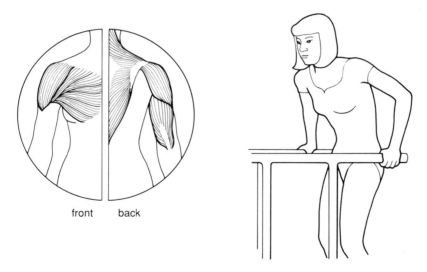

front   back

Parallel Bar Dips

This exercise is excellent for helping you improve your bench press as well as building your triceps. Several equipment manufacturers make parallel bar dip machines that actively assist you with the movement.

◆   THE TECHNIQUE   Support yourself between the parallel bars on your fully extended arms (Figure 7–11). Lower yourself by slowly bending your elbows until your chest is almost even with the bars. Then push up until you reach the starting position. A good way to improve if you can't do any repetitions initially is to have someone hold your waist and assist you during the motion.

Triceps Extension, Nautilus Multitriceps Machine

As effective as the Nautilus curl machine for the biceps, the multitriceps machine is excellent for isolating the triceps muscle.

◆   THE TECHNIQUE   Adjust the seat so that when you sit down, your elbows are slightly lower than your shoulders (Figure 7–12). Place your elbows on the support cushion and your forearms on bar pads (starting position). Extend your elbows as much as possible, then return to the starting position.

Figure 7–12 Nautilus multitriceps machine

Muscles developed: triceps

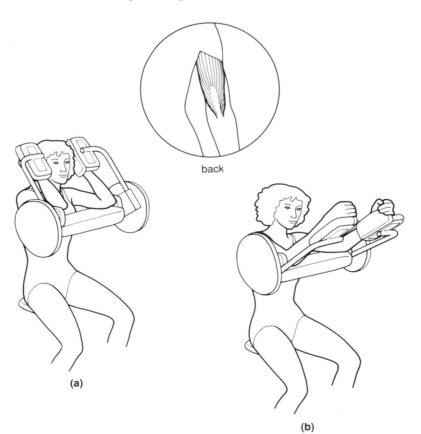

back

(a)

(b)

EXERCISES FOR THE FOREARM

The forearm muscles are essential to any activity requiring that you rapidly snap your wrist, such as golf, the tennis serve, badminton, and throwing a ball. Weakness of the forearm muscles results in tennis or carpenter's elbow. The forearm muscles are also largely responsible for grip strength. Exercises that develop the forearm muscles include wrist curls and wrist rollers.

Wrist Curls

Wrist curls are done using either a pronated or supinated grip. Pronated, or reverse, wrist curls build the wrist extensors, the muscles injured in tennis elbow. Supinated wrist curls build the forearm flexors and are important accessory exercises to biceps curls.

◆   THE TECHNIQUE   You can do this exercise with either a barbell or dumbbells. In a seated position, with forearms resting on your thigh and hands extending over your knees, use a supinated grip to lower the weight as far as possible, then lift your hands upward by bending at the wrists as much as you can (Figure 7–13). Repeat this exercise using a pronated grip. Wrist curls can be done on the Universal Gym using the low pulley station with either the handles or small bar.

A variation of this exercise is the lateral wrist curl. It requires the use of a small bar with the weight affixed at one end. Do the exercise in the same manner as the wrist curl, except bend your wrist to the side.

Wrist Rollers

This exercise requires a machine, such as the wrist roller station on the Universal Gym, or a wrist roller device. The device can be purchased or constructed. To make one, drill a hole through a cylindrical piece of wood and tie a three-foot piece of rope or small chain to it. Then attach the weight to the other end of the rope.

◆   THE TECHNIQUE   While holding the piece of wood out in front of you with both hands, use a pronated grip to lift the weight by winding the rope around the wood (Figure 7–14).

Wrist Rollers, Universal Gym

The wrist roller station on the Universal Gym is much easier to use than the wrist roller device. You can do wrist curls (wrist rollers), reverse wrist curls (reverse wrist rollers), forearm supination (turn palms up), forearm pronation (turn palms down), and lateral wrist curls.

Figure 7–13 Wrist curls: (a) extension, (b) flexion, and (c) using two dumbbells at once

Muscles developed, wrist extension: extensor carpi radialis longus, extensor carpi radialis brevis, extensor carpi ulnaris

Muscles developed, wrist flexion: flexor carpi radialis, flexor carpi ulnaris

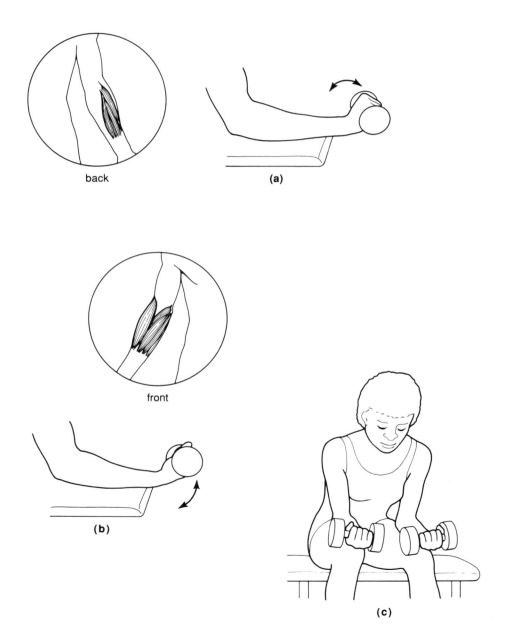

back

(a)

front

(b)

(c)

Figure 7–14 Wrist rollers

Muscles developed: flexor carpi radialis, flexor carpi ulnaris

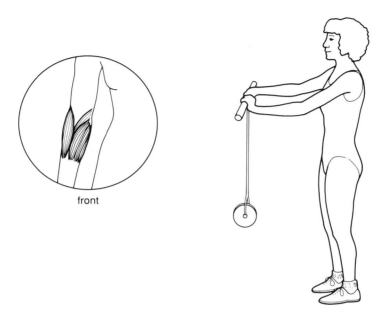

front

◆   THE TECHNIQUE   To do wrist rollers on the Universal Gym, place both hands on the grips and turn the handles clockwise (forward) (Figure 7–15). When your palms are facing up, this exercise builds the muscles on the front of your forearms. Reverse wrist rollers are the same, except you turn the handles counterclockwise.

Other Exercises for the Forearm and Grip

Grip strength is very important in certain sports—tennis, softball, and rock climbing, for example. People often don't have very good grips because they don't work to develop them. Serious weight-trained athletes have very strong forearms and grips. Yet few of them do wrist rollers or wrist curls. Large-muscle weight lifts, such as cleans, snatches, and dead-lifts, place considerable stress on the forearms and hands. If you do those kinds of lifts, you will develop a good grip and strong forearms—especially if you do these lifts without lifting straps. (Straps are cloth or leather belts that you wrap around your hands and the bar to improve grip strength.)

If you don't want to do these exercises, carry around a small rubber ball and squeeze it every time it occurs to you. This isometric exercise is very effective for developing grip and forearm strength.

Figure 7–15 Wrist curls on the Universal Gym

Muscles developed, wrist extension (a, b): extensor carpi radialis longus, extensor carpi radialis brevis, extensor carpi ulnaris

Muscles developed, wrist flexion (c, d): flexor carpi radialis, flexor carpi ulnaris

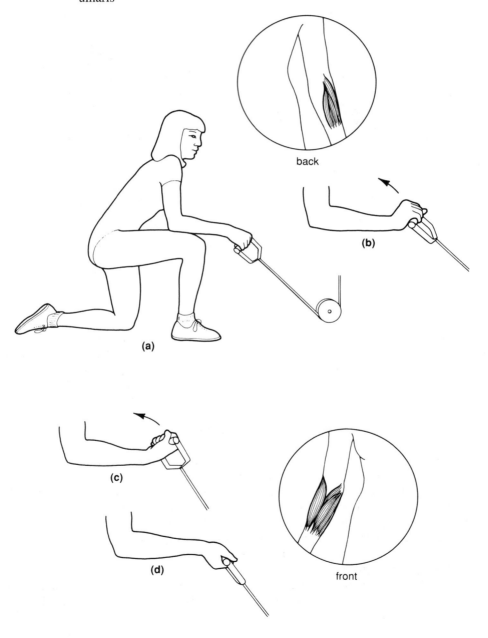

CHAPTER

8 Developing the Neck and Back

MOST PEOPLE HAVE TROUBLE WITH THEIR NECK AND BACK AT SOME POINT DURING THEIR lifetime, yet this part of the body is often neglected by women weight trainers.

The spine is composed of a series of bones called "vertebrae," with the spinal cord running through a channel in these bones. In between the vertebrae lie shock absorbers, the "intervertebral disks." The vertebral column has three natural curves, which aid the disks in absorbing shock. Strong muscles are important for maintaining these curves.

Weight trainers must take special care to select exercises that do not damage the intervertebral disks. Nerves emerge from the spinal cord and act as messengers between the tissues and the central nervous system. Pain and muscle spasm result if abnormal pressure is put on these nerves. Strong neck and back muscles help to maintain proper alignment in the vertebrae, preventing injury to the disks and pressure on the spinal nerves.

Strong neck and back muscles are also critical for movement. Because the neck controls the movement of the head, strong neck muscles are important in any sport. The middle and upper back muscles are also vital in almost all movements and provide a balance to the muscles of the front of the body. The lower back muscles help maintain the body in an upright posture and are important in bending movements. Because the lower back is notoriously vulnerable to injury, it is necessary to keep these muscles strong and flexible.

The following exercises are divided into three parts—exercises for the neck, the upper back, and the lower back. Considerable overlap exists among these areas, and exercises described in other parts of the book often affect the neck and back.

EXERCISES FOR THE NECK

Strong neck muscles are important for all active people. Most people do not follow a systematic program for strengthening the neck muscles, even though the neck is vulnerable to serious injury. Neck pain affects many women, often because of poor strength in the neck and upper back muscles. Including basic neck-strengthening exercises in the weight training program could help prevent neck injuries.

The intensity of neck exercise should be increased gradually, particularly if you are recovering from a neck injury or have neck pain. Neck muscles are relatively small and thus more susceptible than larger muscles to the destructive effects of sudden overload.

There are three basic techniques for strengthening the neck:

◆ Manual-resistance exercises

◆ Neck harness exercises

◆ Nautilus four-way neck machine

Manual Exercises

Manual-resistance neck exercises provide an exercise load in all neck motions. These techniques are an easy, inexpensive way to strengthen neck muscles and can be incorporated almost anywhere in the program. For example, they can be added to your stretching routine prior to running or included as one of your weight training exercises.

CAUTION   ◆   Extreme care is essential: manual resistance can be very dangerous if excessive force is used. Have your physical therapist, doctor, or coach instruct you in proper technique before attempting these exercises!

Do these exercises on only one side of the body at a time. Do not cross the body's midline. Three movements should be used in your manual-resistance neck training program: flexion, extension, and lateral flexion. Neck flexion is when you bring your chin toward your chest; neck extension is when you tilt from a flexed to neutral position; and neck lateral flexion is when you tilt your head to the side. Do not hyperextend the neck (i.e., extend the head backward past the midline of the body) because this could cause injury.

◆   THE TECHNIQUE   Manual neck flexion (Figure 8–1): Lie on your back on a table, with your head hanging over the edge. Have your training partner supply resistance to your forehead as you attempt to bring your chin to your chest. Resistance should be minimal when you first start doing this exercise.

◆   THE TECHNIQUE   Manual neck extension (Figure 8–2): Lie on your stomach on a bench with your head hanging over the edge. Have your training partner supply resistance to the back of your head as you attempt to bring it toward the back of your spine. Again, extend your head only to the midline of your body.

Figure 8–1 Manual neck flexion

Muscles developed: sternocleidomastoideus, scaleni

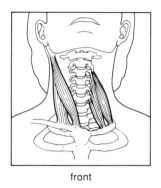

front

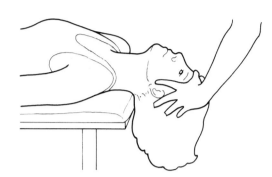

Figure 8–2 Manual neck extension

Muscles developed: splenius capitus, splenius cervicus, trapezius

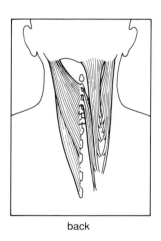

back

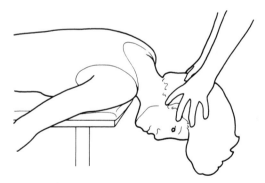

◆   THE TECHNIQUE   Manual neck lateral flexion (Figure 8–3): Lie on your side on a table with your head hanging over the edge. Have your training partner supply resistance to the side of your head as you attempt to bring your ear to your shoulder. Do this exercise on the right and left sides of your body.

Note: You can provide manual resistance to yourself by pushing on the front, back, or side of your head as you perform the various neck movements.

Figure 8–3 Manual neck lateral flexion

Muscles developed: sternocleidomastoideus, scaleni

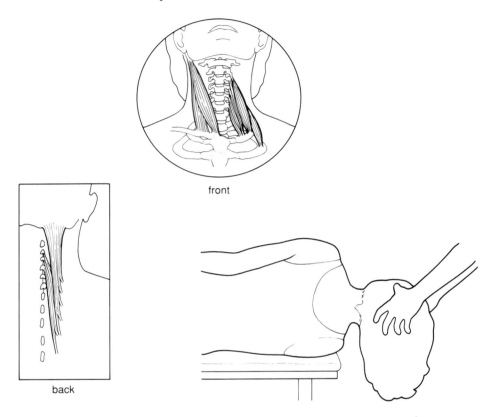

front

back

Neck Harness Exercises

Neck harness exercises involve the same movements as manual-resistance neck exercises, except the resistance is provided by weights suspended from a neck harness rather than by a training partner. Neck harnesses are relatively inexpensive and can be purchased at almost any sporting goods store.

Neck exercises for the Universal Gym are identical to the neck harness exercises presented in this chapter. The only difference between the two is that the Universal Gym neck harness is attached to the neck conditioning station, while the free-weight neck harness is attached to weight plates. The neck harness provides resistance to the neck during neck flexion, extension, and lateral flexion.

◆   THE TECHNIQUE   Neck flexion (Figure 8–4): Wearing the neck harness with weight suspended from the harness chain, lie on your back on a table. Allow your head to

Figure 8–4 Neck flexion with harness

Muscles developed: sternocleidomastoideus, scaleni

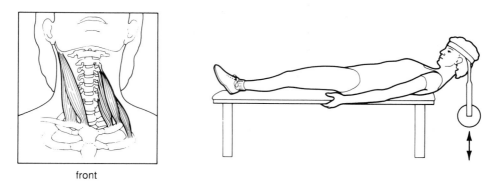

front

Figure 8–5 Neck extension with harness

Muscles developed: splenius capitus, splenius cervicus, trapezius

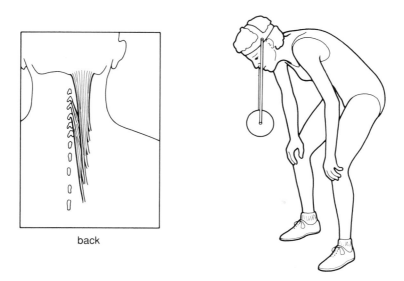

back

slowly roll backward, then pull the weight back up by moving your chin toward your chest. Make sure to hold the sides of the table with your hands so you don't lose your balance.

◆   THE TECHNIQUE   Neck extension (Figure 8–5): Wearing the neck harness with weight suspended from the harness chain, stand with your knees bent and hands on your thighs. Slowly lower the weight with your neck as far as possible, then return to the starting position.

◆   THE TECHNIQUE   Neck lateral flexion: Wearing the neck harness with weight suspended from the harness chain, lie on your side on a table. Allow your head to slowly bend to the lower side, then pull the weight upward by moving your ear toward your higher shoulder. Do this exercise on the right and left sides of your body.

◆   THE TECHNIQUE   Neck lateral flexion, Universal Gym (Figure 8–6): Stand with the side of your face exposed to the neck machine. Put the harness on your head and attach the fastener to the neck conditioning station. Stand far enough away from the machine so that you feel tension on the harness. Bend your head toward your outer shoulder.

Neck Machine Exercises

Several equipment manufacturers make neck exercise machines that provide resistance during flexion, extension, and lateral flexion. Nautilus makes a neck rotation machine, but

Figure 8–6 Lateral neck flexion, Universal Gym

Muscles developed: sternocleidomastoideus, scaleni

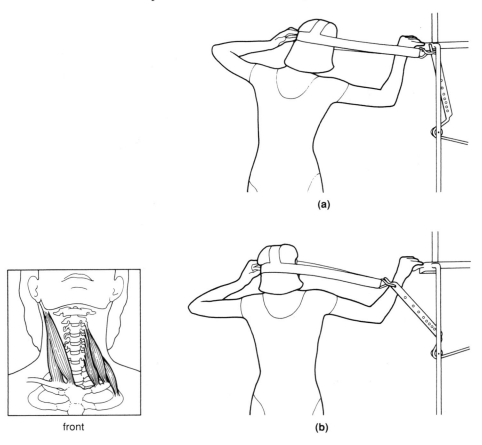

(a)

front   (b)

few facilities have it. Working out with neck machines is probably superior to performing the manual or neck harness methods, so use the machines if you have access to them.

Four-way Neck Machine, Nautilus, Eagle

These machines allow you to do neck flexion, extension, and lateral flexion. Each movement requires you to change your seating position. Take care to do the exercises with your neck muscles, not your trunk.

CAUTION ◆ Progress slowly. Neck muscles are easily strained and take a long time to heal. Do not do these exercises if they cause sharp pain. Do not hyperextend the neck.

◆ THE TECHNIQUE   Flexion (Figure 8–7a): Adjust the seat so that your forehead rests in the center of the two pads (starting position). Bend your head forward as far as possible, then return to the starting position.

◆ THE TECHNIQUE   Extension (Figure 8–7b): Adjust the seat so that the back of your head rests in the center of the two pads (starting position). Bend your head backward as far as possible, then return to the starting position.

◆ THE TECHNIQUE   Lateral flexion (Figure 8–7c): Adjust the seat so that the side of your head rests in the center of the two pads (starting position). Bend your head sideward toward your shoulder as far as possible, then return to the starting position. Do the exercise on the right and left sides of your head.

EXERCISES FOR THE UPPER BACK: THE TRAPS

In the upper back the two muscles most important for movement are the trapezius and the latissimus dorsi, which weight trainers refer to as the "traps" and "lats." As with other parts of the body, many of the exercises presented in this book will develop the upper back, but the following exercises are good for specifically training the "traps":

   ◆ Shoulder shrugs
   ◆ Nautilus neck and shoulder machine
   ◆ Rowing exercise

The traps are also developed when you do overhead presses, upright rowing (see chapter 6), and pulling exercises (e.g., cleans, snatches, and high pulls; see chapter 10). If you are doing these exercises, you probably don't need to do anything additional for this muscle.

Figure 8–7 Neck flexion (Eagle), extension, lateral flexion on Nautilus machine

Muscles developed, flexion: sternocleidomastoideus, scaleni

Muscles developed, lateral flexion: sternocleidomastoideus, scaleni

Muscles developed, extension: splenius capitus, splenius cervicus, trapezius

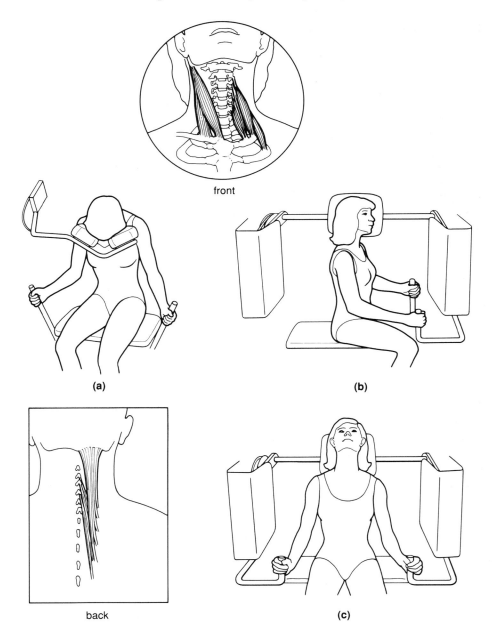

front

(a)   (b)

back   (c)

Shoulder Shrugs

Shoulder shrugs can be done with a barbell or commercially manufactured shoulder shrug machines. Be careful not to cheat on this exercise — it's easy to let your legs initiate the movement.

◆   THE TECHNIQUE   In a standing position, hold a barbell with a pronated grip, hands shoulder-width apart, arms extended, and the weight resting below your waist (Figure 8–8). Without bending your elbows, lift your shoulders toward your head, rotate your shoulders back, then return to the starting position.

Figure 8–8 Shoulder shrugs

Muscles developed: trapezius, rhomboids, deltoid

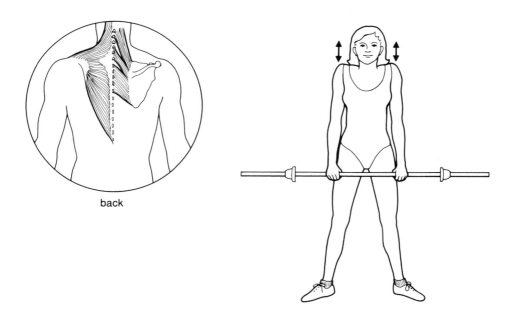

back

Shoulder Shrugs, Universal Gym

◆   THE TECHNIQUE   Remove the bench from the bench press station on the Universal Gym (Figure 8–9). Face the machine, grasp the handles with arms extended, and lift the bar to your waist (starting position). Without bending your elbows, lift your shoulders toward your head, rotate your shoulders back, then return to the starting position.

Figure 8–9 Shoulder shrugs, Universal Gym

Muscles developed: trapezius, rhomboids, deltoid

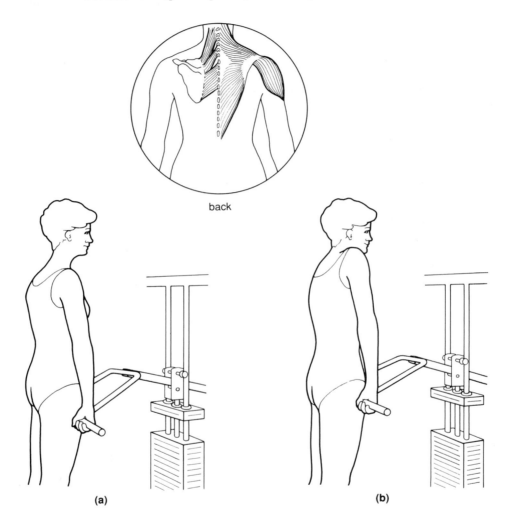

back

(a)   (b)

Neck and Shoulder Machine (Shoulder Shrugs), Nautilus

The Nautilus neck and shoulder machine is an excellent way to do shoulder shrugs because it is not limited by the strength of your grip (you don't hold onto a bar).

◆   THE TECHNIQUE   Sit facing the machine and place your forearms through the support pads with palms up (starting position). With elbows flexed, shrug your shoulders toward your head, then return to the starting position (Figure 8–10).

Figure 8–10 Nautilus neck and shoulder (shoulder shrug) machine

Muscles developed: trapezius, rhomboids, deltoid

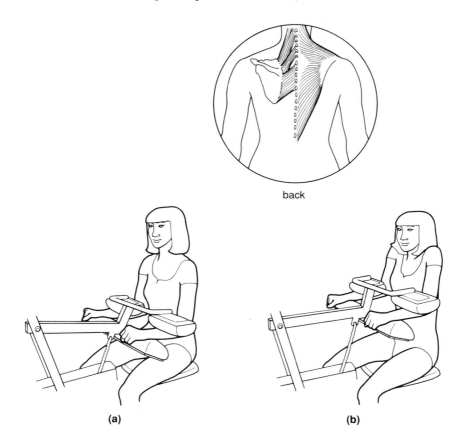

back

(a)   (b)

Bent-over Rowing

Upright rowing was described in chapter 6 as a good shoulder exercise. In addition to working the major muscles of the upper back, bent-over rowing also works the shoulders.

◆   THE TECHNIQUE   Bend at the waist with knees bent and arms extended, holding a barbell or dumbbell (Figure 8–11). Lift the weight to your chest, then return to the starting position. The shoulder blades should move together as the arms pull back; otherwise, the biceps do most of the work.

CAUTION   ◆   This exercise may place excessive pressure on your intervertebral disks, so don't do it if you have back trouble.

Figure 8–11 Bent-over rowing

Muscles developed: trapezius, rhomboids, posterior deltoid, biceps, latissimus dorsi

front   back

(a)

(b)

Bent-over Rowing, Universal Gym

◆   THE TECHNIQUE   Using the low pulley station on the Universal Gym, face the machine and bend forward at the waist, keeping your back straight (starting position). Stand far enough away from the machine so that you can extend your arms (Figure 8–12). Using either the small bar or the handles, pull the weight toward your chest, then return to the starting position.

EXERCISES FOR THE UPPER BACK: THE LATS

The latissimus dorsi (the ''lats'') move the arms downward, backward, and inward. They are used in the tennis serve and when throwing a ball. A variety of exercises already

Figure 8–12 Bent-over rowing, Universal Gym

Muscles developed: trapezius, latissimus dorsi, posterior deltoid, biceps, rhomboids

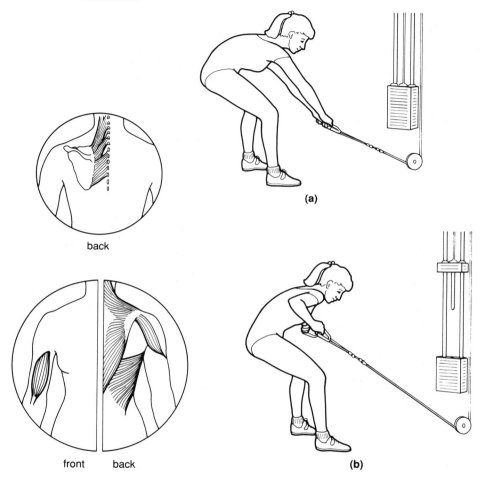

back

front   back

(a)

(b)

discussed work the lats, including pullovers, Nautilus pullover machine, parallel bar dips, and bent-over rowing, but the following two exercises are particularly effective:

◆ Pull-ups (pull-ups, chin-ups, and behind-the-neck pull-ups)
◆ Lat pulls

Pull-ups

Pull-ups are extremely effective exercises for building the lats and other upper body muscles. You can do them wherever you find a bar on which to pull yourself up — there are pull-up bars in any gymnasium or playground — or you can purchase one that can be mounted in a doorway. The three variations of this exercise are pull-ups, chin-ups, and behind-the-neck pull-ups. If you can't do this exercise at first, have a spotter hold you at the waist and assist you with the movement. And don't worry — you'll be able to do unassisted pull-ups in a short time.

◆ THE TECHNIQUE   Pull-ups (Figure 8–13a): Hang from a bar, elbows fully extended, using a pronated grip, with hands slightly more than shoulder-width apart. Pull yourself up until your chin passes the bar, then return to the starting position. Do not swing your legs during this exercise, and be sure to fully extend your elbows after each repetition.

Figure 8–13 (a) Pull-ups, (b) chin-ups, and (c) behind-the-neck pull-ups

Muscles developed: latissimus dorsi, biceps

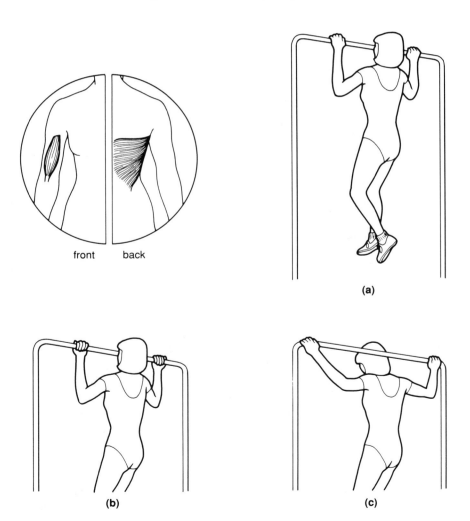

front   back

(a)

(b)   (c)

◆   THE TECHNIQUE   Chin-ups (Figure 8–13b): This exercise is identical to pull-ups except that you use a supinated grip. Chin-ups are easier, however, so they are good to do if you have difficulty with the other forms of this exercise. Chin-ups are excellent for building the biceps.

◆   THE TECHNIQUE   Behind-the-neck pull-ups (Figure 8–13c): This exercise places more stress on the lats and is much more difficult than the other kinds of pull-ups. Hang from a bar, using a pronated grip, with hands apart as far as possible. Pull yourself up until the back of your neck makes contact with the bar, then return to the starting position.

Lat Pulls on Universal, Nautilus, or Other Lat Machine

Lat pulls require the use of a lat machine. They are very similar to pull-ups, except that you pull weights down instead of pulling your body weight up. They also develop the muscles on the front of your arm (biceps). To emphasize the lats, do the exercise using a wide grip; to work the biceps more, use a narrower grip.

◆   THE TECHNIQUE   From a seated or kneeling position, grasp the bar of the lat machine with arms fully extended (Figure 8–14). Pull the weight down until it reaches the back of your neck, then return to the starting position.

CAUTION   ◆   Take care not to touch your neck bones with the bar; you could injure them if you mistakenly bang them too hard.

Figure 8–14 Lat pulls

Muscles developed: latissimus dorsi, biceps

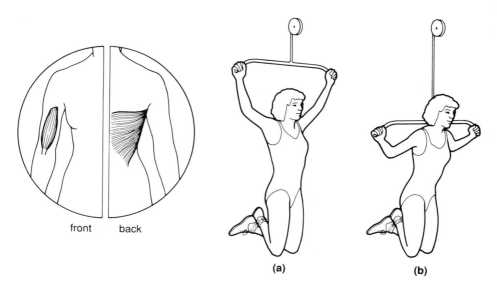

front   back

(a)   (b)

As you get stronger, you may need a spotter to hold you down during the exercise because the weight you use may pull you up (Figure 8–15). The spotter should get behind you and place her hands firmly on your shoulders.

Figure 8–15 Spotting during lat pull exercise

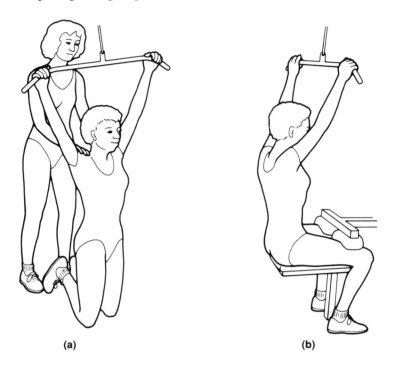

(a)   (b)

CAUTION ◆ The spotter must take great care to keep her head away from the bar; it could hit her if the lifter suddenly let go of it.

◆ THE TECHNIQUE   Lat pull machine, Nautilus (Figure 8–16): Adjust the seat so that your arms can be fully extended. Strap yourself in with the seat belt, extend your arms, and grasp the handles of the small bar (starting position). Pull the bar to your collar bone, then return to the starting position.

EXERCISES FOR THE LOWER BACK

More than 85 percent of the population experiences back pain during their lifetime. Experts attribute some of this to lack of strength and flexibility in the spinal muscles. An ideal exercise program for the lower back would build strong and flexible back muscles to help you achieve optimal spinal alignment and minimize pressure on the spinal nerves. Unfor-

Figure 8–16 Lat pull, Nautilus machine

Muscles developed: latissimus dorsi, biceps

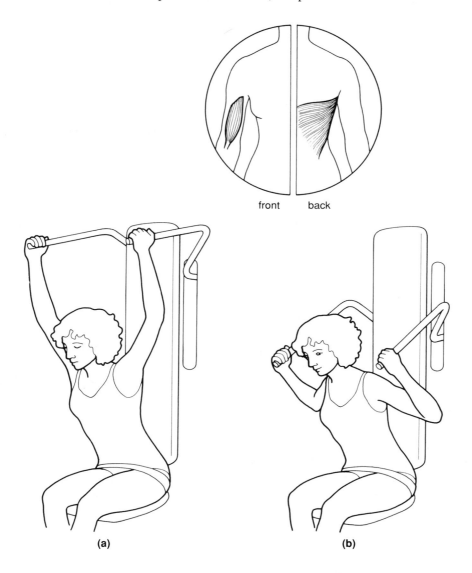

(a)   (b)

tunately, the best exercises for strengthening the low-back muscles are often the same exercises that place the most stress on the spinal disks. The low-back muscles are well suited for maintaining an erect posture, but poorly suited for lifting heavy objects. Therefore, proper lifting techniques are absolutely essential when working the lower back. (These techniques were discussed in chapter 5.)

Other factors important to a healthy back include strong abdominal and leg muscles and flexible leg muscles. Regular aerobic exercise is also thought to help prevent back pain.

Three types of low-back exercises are discussed in the next section:

◆ Isometric extension exercises

◆ Specific low-back weight training exercises

◆ Exercises having a secondary effect on the muscles of the lower back

No low-back program is right for everyone. If an exercise causes pain, stop doing it and seek professional advice. Circumstances change; an exercise that is inappropriate for you now may be all right six months from now after a period of conditioning.

Isometric Spine Extension Exercises

The purpose of isometric spine extension exercises is to strengthen the low-back muscles so that they are better able to maintain spinal alignment. These exercises are very good for helping you stabilize your spine, which most back experts feel is the key to a pain-free back. Two exercises in this category include:

◆ Unilateral spine extensions

◆ Bilateral spine extensions

◆   THE TECHNIQUE   Unilateral spine extensions (Figure 8–17a): Balance on your right hand and knee. Extend your left leg to the rear, and reach forward with your left arm. Hold this position for ten to thirty seconds. Repeat with your right leg and right arm. Start with 5 repetitions and advance to 15. You can make this exercise more challenging by attaching weights to your legs and arms. Ankle and wrist weights are inexpensive and can be purchased at any sporting goods store.

◆   THE TECHNIQUE   Bilateral spine extensions (Figure 8–17b): Balance on your left hand and right knee. Lift your left leg and right arm. Extend the leg to the rear, and reach to the front with your arm. Hold this position for ten to thirty seconds. Repeat with the opposite arm and leg.

Low-Back Exercises

Weak back muscles are easily injured when you do squats and pulling exercises (e.g., cleans and snatches). So if your weight training program includes these exercises, it's a good idea to add low-back exercises. Three popular ones are back extensions, the good morning exercise, and the Nautilus back extension machine.

Figure 8–17 (a) Unilateral back extensions, (b) bilateral back extensions

Muscles developed: sacrospinalis, gluteus maximus

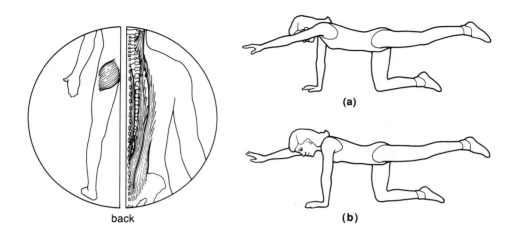

back (a) (b)

CAUTION ◆ Low-back weight training exercises may subject the spinal disks to considerable pressure. If you suffer from lower back pain, these exercises may do more harm than good. Straight-leg dead-lifts, although very popular, are not recommended at all.

Back Extensions, Universal Gym or Back Extension Machine

Back extensions are also often called "back hyperextensions." However, it is not a good idea to extend too far backward—you could put too much pressure on the spinal disks.

◆ THE TECHNIQUE Lie face down on a back extension bench with your upper body extending over the edge (Figure 8–18). Hang down as far as you can, then lift your torso until it is again aligned with your legs. This exercise can also be done on a bench if you have a spotter hold your legs down.

The Good Morning Exercise

This is a particularly good accessory exercise to a program containing squats and pulling exercises.

Figure 8–18 Back extensions on Universal Gym

Muscles developed: sacrospinalis

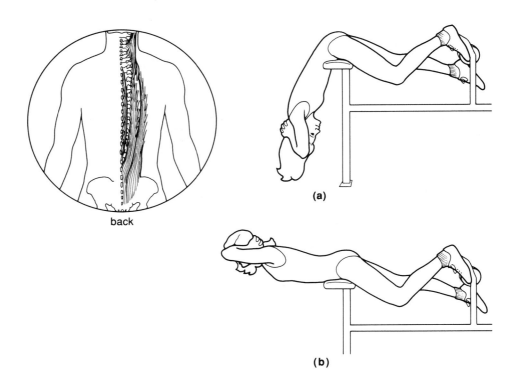

back

(a)

(b)

◆ THE TECHNIQUE Standing, place a barbell on your shoulders and flex your knees slightly (starting position). Bend at the waist while keeping your head up as much as possible, then return to the starting position (Figure 8–19). Do this exercise slowly and smoothly, and add weight very gradually. In general do more repetitions (10–20) and use less weight than you normally would for other weight training exercises.

Low-Back Machine, Nautilus

◆ THE TECHNIQUE Sit on the seat and place your upper legs under the large thigh-support pads, your back on the back roller pad, and your feet planted firmly on the platform (starting position). Placing your hands on your abdomen, extend backward until your back is straight, then return to the starting position (Figure 8–20).

Figure 8–19 The good morning exercise

Muscles developed: sacrospinalis

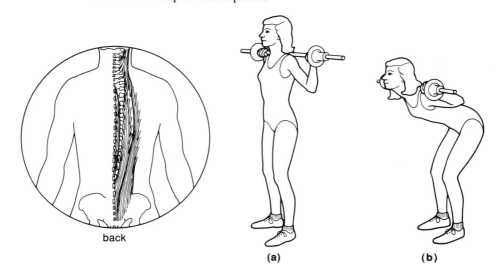

back

(a)   (b)

Figure 8–20 Nautilus back machine

Muscles developed: sacrospinalis

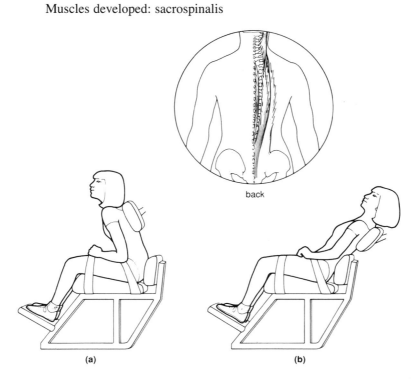

back

(a)   (b)

Exercises with a Secondary Effect on the Lower Back

Because the lower back is used to stabilize the upper body during many activities, almost all weight training exercises stress the low-back muscles to a certain extent. Exercises such as squats, cleans, and snatches are particularly good at developing low-back strength.

CAUTION   ◆   Because these lifts actively involve the back, it is particularly important to protect the back by wearing a weight lifting belt and observing proper lifting techniques.

C H A P T E R

9 Developing the Abdominal Muscles

MOST WOMEN WANT A FLAT STOMACH. WELL, HERE'S SOME GOOD NEWS AND SOME BAD news. No matter how much exercise you do, fat around the middle will remain unless you burn up more calories than you take in. There is no such thing as spot reducing — you can't exercise muscles and lose the fat that lies over them.

Now, for the good news. The abdominal muscles are the major supporting structures of the abdomen. Unlike the legs and arms, which have large bones that provide structure, the abdomen has no bones. Strong muscles support the area and act like a biological girdle to "hold you in." If you strengthen the abdominal muscles, the area will look tighter, even though the fat may still be there.

The principal abdominal muscles include the rectus abdominis, which causes the trunk to bend, and the obliques, which assist the rectus and allow you to rotate your trunk and bend to the side.

There are many abdominal exercises, but a good number of these pose a danger to the neck and lower back and should be avoided. Dangerous abdominal exercises include Roman chair sit-ups (Figure 9–1a), straight-leg sit-ups (Figure 9–1b), double-leg lifts, and sit-ups with hands behind the head.

CAUTION ◆ Roman chair sit-ups, straight-leg sit-ups, and double-leg lifts place excessive stress on the intervertebral disks. Performing sit-ups with hands behind the head could injure the neck.

Doing a few sets of these dangerous exercises will probably not cause immediate injury. Doing them for many years could stress the disks, which could eventually lead to

Figure 9–1 Dangerous abdominal exercises: (a) Roman chair sit-ups, (b) straight-leg sit-ups

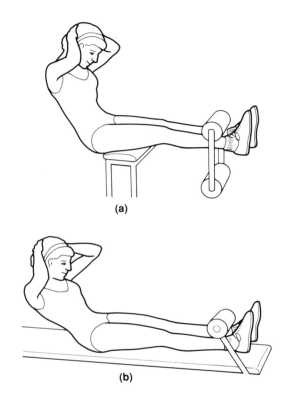

(a)

(b)

disk deterioration and chronic back and neck pain. The best practice is to avoid exercises that may cause problems.

Many exercises are effective for building the muscles of the trunk, including the following:

- ◆ Isometric abdominal exercise
- ◆ Crunches
- ◆ Sit-ups
- ◆ Nautilus abdominal machine
- ◆ Hanging knee raises
- ◆ Reverse beetles
- ◆ Nautilus hip flexion
- ◆ Twists
- ◆ Nautilus rotary torso machine

ABDOMINAL AND HIP FLEXOR EXERCISES

Isometric Abdominal Exercise

Perhaps you're not aware that you have your own built-in abdominal exercise machine. You can work on your abdominal muscles anytime, anywhere.

◆   THE TECHNIQUE   To do the isometric abdominal exercise, simply tighten your abdominal muscles for ten to thirty seconds. In other words, hold your stomach in. If you do this periodically throughout the day, you will notice a difference within a few weeks. But don't hold your breath while doing it, because this could restrict blood flow to the heart.

Crunches

Sports scientists have discovered that the abdominal muscles can get a tremendous workout by moving through a very small range of motion. You don't need to do full sit-ups to develop fully trained abdominals. Crunches have been found to be just as effective, and they place much less stress on the back.

◆   THE TECHNIQUE   Lie on your back on the floor (Figure 9–2). Place your feet on the floor or on a bench, or extend your legs up against a wall. With arms folded across your chest, curl your trunk upward by raising your head and shoulders from the ground. Your back should remain stationary. Resistance can be increased by holding a weight plate on your chest.

Figure 9–2 Crunches (abdominal curls)

Muscles developed: rectus abdominus

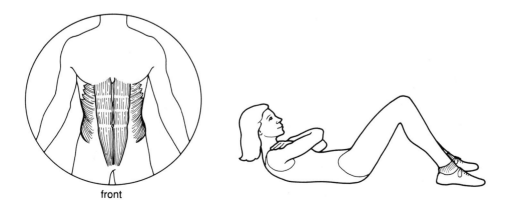

front

Sit-ups

Sit-ups are a basic exercise in almost everyone's program. Thirty years ago, sit-ups were done with straight legs. Then it was discovered that straight-leg sit-ups are hard on the back and exercise a large hip flexor muscle group more than the abdominals. Recent studies suggest that doing sit-ups with your hands behind your head may cause neck injuries. Little of the exercise's value is lost by doing it with arms folded across the chest or hands touching the ears. If you insist on doing sit-ups with your hands behind your head, use your hands only to cradle your head — not to help you complete the exercise.

◆   THE TECHNIQUE   Lying on your back with knees bent, feet flat on the floor, and arms folded across the chest, bend at the waist and raise your head and shoulders toward your knees until your hands touch your thighs (Figure 9–3). Return to the starting position. You can modify this exercise to increase the stress on the obliques by twisting on the way up. As with crunches, the resistance can be increased by doing this exercise with weights.

Slantboard Bent-knee Sit-ups, Universal Gym

This exercise can be done on any slantboard made for doing sit-ups. A problem with this exercise is that it's difficult to bend your knees while doing it, particularly as the angle of

Figure 9–3 Sit-ups

Muscles developed: rectus abdominus, obliques

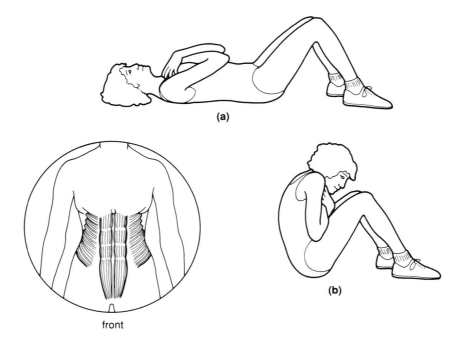

(a)

(b)

front

the board increases. As with regular sit-ups, you should not put your hands behind your head. (This is even more important when you're using a slantboard.)

◆   THE TECHNIQUE   Set the board at an angle that allows you to maintain bent knees throughout the exercise (Figure 9–4). Start with no slant if you are unsure of your capabilities. With your hands folded across your chest, lie supine on the board, knees bent, and feet firmly anchored under the support cushions or belt (starting position). Bend at the waist and sit up.

CAUTION   ◆   Be sure to do this exercise with your abdominal muscles — don't "rock" your body forward because you could injure your back. Never place your hands behind your head because of the possibility of neck injury.

Abdominal Machine, Nautilus

The Nautilus abdominal machine is very similar to the Nautilus back machine, except you push forward instead of backward.

◆   THE TECHNIQUE   Adjust the seat so that the machine rotates at the level of your navel, the pad rests on your upper chest, and your feet can rest comfortably on the floor

Figure 9–4 Bent-knee sit-ups on Universal Gym slantboard

Muscles developed: rectus abdominus, obliques

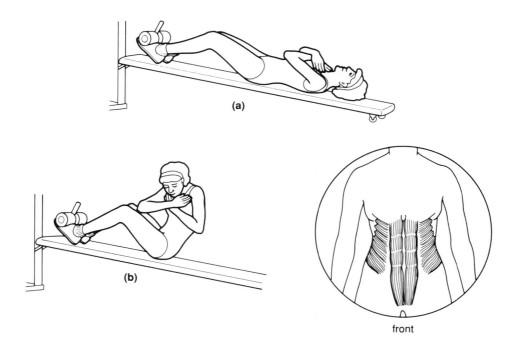

(a)

(b)

front

Figure 9–5 Nautilus abdominal machine

Muscles developed: rectus abdominus

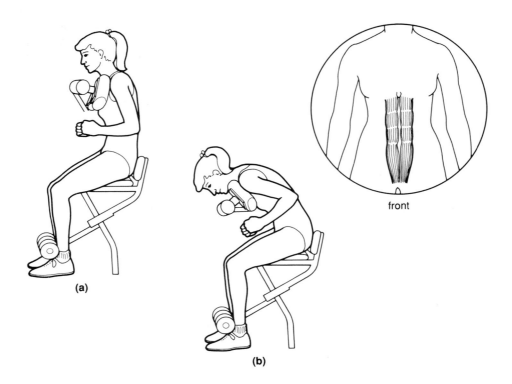

(a)

(b)

front

(starting position). Move your trunk forward as much as possible, then return to the starting position (Figure 9–5).

Hanging Knee Raises

This exercise is done hanging from a bar, between two bars, or on the hip flexor station of the Universal Gym. It is a good exercise for the abdominal and hip flexor muscles.

◆   THE TECHNIQUE   Hanging from a bar, bring your knees up toward your chest, then return to the starting position (Figure 9–6a, b). You can also do this exercise hanging between two bars, such as can be found on the Universal Gym.

◆   THE TECHNIQUE   Hip flexor machine, Universal Gym (Figure 9–6c, d): On the hip flexor station of the Universal Gym, grasp the handles and rest your forearms on the pads (starting position). Draw your knees toward your chest, then return to the starting position.

Figure 9–6 Hanging knee raises

Muscles developed: rectus abdominus, iliopsoas, quadriceps

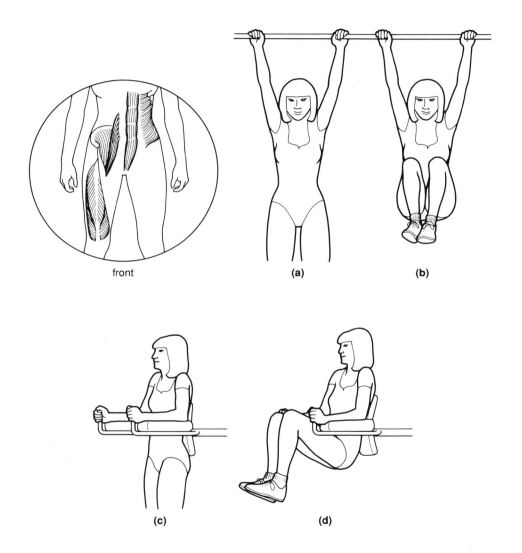

front   (a)   (b)

(c)   (d)

Reverse Beetles

This exercise got its name from the way weight trainers look when they do it — they resemble beetles who have been turned onto their backs. Reverse beetles can be modified to increase the stress on the obliques by twisting as you do them.

Figure 9–7 Reverse beetles

Muscles developed: rectus abdominus, iliopsoas, quadriceps

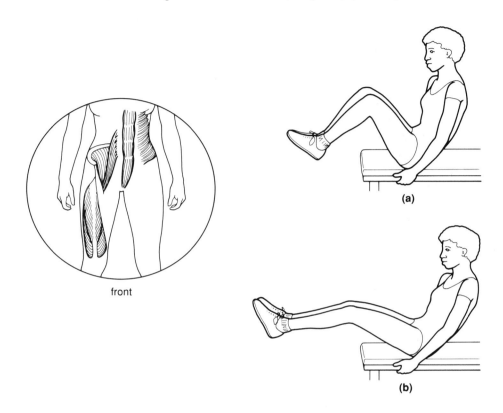

front

(a)

(b)

◆   THE TECHNIQUE   From a seated position on a bench, curl your trunk by bringing knees and shoulders together (Figure 9–7). Then straighten your legs and move your shoulders back.

Hip Flexion Machine, Nautilus

This exercise mainly strengthens the iliopsoas muscle, a hip flexor. However, the abdominal muscles stabilize the trunk, so they get a good workout too. This exercise has many of the same effects as the hanging knee raises and reverse beetles.

◆   THE TECHNIQUE   Sit in the machine and fasten the belt cross the middle of your thighs (Figure 9–8). Then lie on your back with your head resting on the bench and grab the handles behind your head (starting position). Bring your knees to your chest, then return to the starting position.

Figure 9–8 Nautilus hip flexion machine

Muscles developed: rectus abdominus, iliopsoas, quadriceps

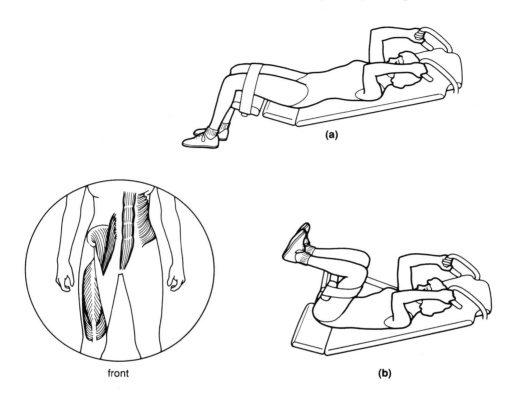

front   (b)

EXERCISES FOR THE OBLIQUES

Twists

Twists are a great way to exercise the obliques. But remember, exercising specific body parts will only help hold in the fat, not get rid of it. This exercise may not be a good idea for people who have back pain.

◆   THE TECHNIQUE   From either a seated or standing position, place a pole on your shoulders and rotate as far as possible, first to the left and then to the right (Figure 9–9). Later, you can use a barbell with weights to get added resistance. If you are more interested in definition than size (as most people are), do many repetitions rather than use a lot of weight.

CAUTION   ◆   Twisting exercises can cause back pain in some people—exercise with caution.

Figure 9–9 Twists

Muscles developed: rectus abdominus, obliques

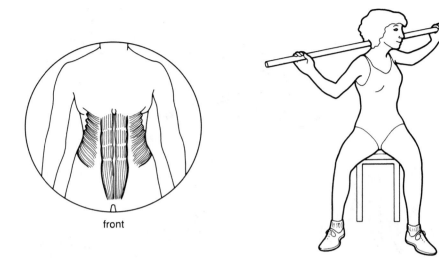

front

Rotary Torso Machine, Nautilus

This is a "high-tech" twist machine. There are two sides to this machine — one to rotate your trunk clockwise and the other to work your trunk counterclockwise.

◆   THE TECHNIQUE   Sit on the right-hand seat and grasp the handles (Figure 9–10). Push with your right hand and rotate your trunk to the left. After completing your repetitions, sit on the left-hand seat, grasp the handles, push with your left hand, and rotate your trunk to the right.

Figure 9–10 Rotary torso machine, Nautilus

Muscles developed: internal and external obliques, rectus abdominus

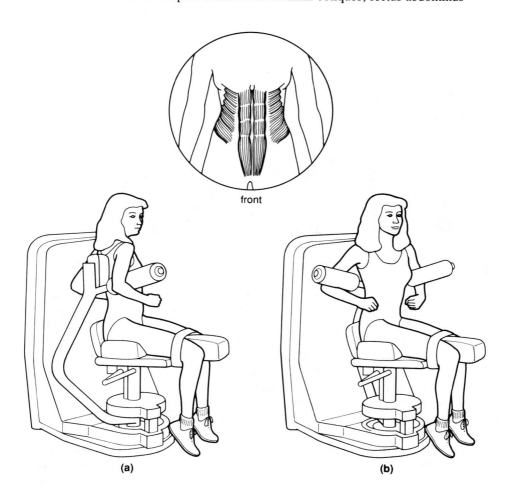

front

(a)   (b)

C H A P T E R

10 Developing the Lower Body

WOMEN CARRY MOST OF THEIR MUSCLE MASS IN THE LOWER BODY, THE LEG MUSCLES being the body's largest and most powerful muscles. Most athletic movements require that power be initiated with the leg and hip muscles. For example, golfers and tennis players initiate movement with their legs and finish the movement with their upper bodies. Those failing to use the lower body effectively, relying instead on the weaker and more fragile upper body muscles, perform inefficiently and are more prone to injury.

Figure 10–1 shows the basic athletic position used in sports such as tennis, racket-ball, and volleyball. The legs are bent and the center of gravity is low. The person can easily move in any direction and has good stability. Movement is much easier and more effective if the lower body muscles are strong and powerful.

This chapter describes exercises for developing strength, power, and muscle shape in the lower body: multijoint exercises, accessory leg-strengthening exercises, and advanced lifts. You will have stronger, more defined legs if you include some of these exercises in your program.

MULTIJOINT LOWER BODY EXERCISES

Multijoint exercises involve movement in two or more joints. Squats and leg presses are multijoint exercises that develop strength in the lower body, which can improve performance in most sports. They also increase strength, to a certain extent, in the back and abdominal muscles. Exercises included in this category are:

- ◆ Squats
- ◆ Power rack squats

Figure 10–1 Basic athletic position

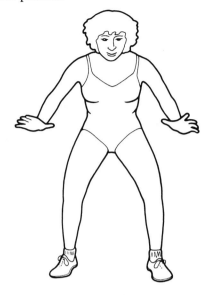

- ◆ Leg presses (Universal Gym and Nautilus)
- ◆ Front squats
- ◆ Hack squats
- ◆ Lunges

Squats (Knee Bends)

People often avoid squats because of reports that deep knee bends overstretch the knee ligaments. In fact, you can squat very low before the knee ligaments are stretched significantly. Good form is essential in this lift. Beginners very often use too much weight; consequently, they bend their backs too much during the lift and sometimes injure themselves.

◆   THE TECHNIQUE   Most experts recommend using a weight-lifting belt when doing squats (Figure 10–2). Begin the exercise standing with your feet shoulder-width apart and toes pointed slightly outward. Rest the bar on the back of your shoulders, your hands holding it in that position. Keep your head up and your lower back straight. Squat down (under control) until your thighs are approximately parallel with the floor and gluteals are about one inch below the knee. Drive upward toward the starting position, keeping your back in a fixed position throughout the exercise. A general strategy for this lift is to go down slow and come up fast.

CAUTION   ◆   Never "bounce" at the bottom of the squat — this could injure the ligaments of your knee.

Figure 10–2 The squat

Muscles developed: quadriceps, gluteus maximus, sacrospinalis

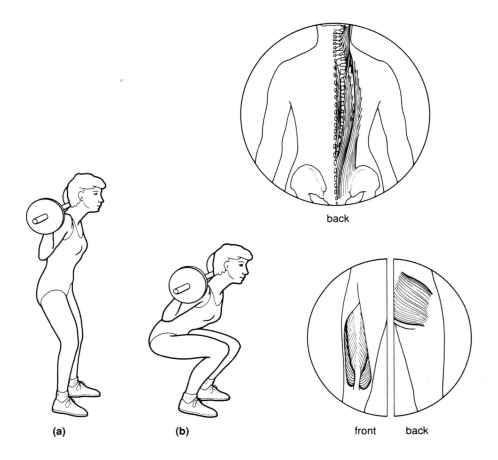

back

(a)   (b)   front   back

Safety should be of primary concern. A good squat rack is an important prerequisite. The rack should be sturdy and adjustable for people of different heights. Some racks have a safety bar at the bottom that can be used if the lift cannot be completed. Two spotters are also required — one standing on each side of the lifter, prepared to assist in case she fails to complete a repetition. Weight belts are recommended. Some people wrap their knees and use weight-lifting boots to provide added support.

You can do many variations of this exercise to increase squatting power, such as power rack squats and bench squats. Because of the high risk of injury, however, we do not recommend bench squats.

CAUTION ◆ Bench squats can be dangerous: you may unintentionally slam down on the bench and injure your spine.

Power Rack Squats

Power rack squats allow you to use the power rack to overcome sticking points in the range of motion of the squat exercise. As with the power rack bench press described in chapter 6, you select three positions along the range of motion and work out at each one.

◆   THE TECHNIQUE   The bar should be placed on the first pair of pegs so that it is resting on your shoulders and your thighs are nearly parallel with the ground (Figure 10–3). Push the weight upward until you are standing upright. After your workout at the first position, move the pegs so that the bar lies in the middle of the range of motion. Repeat the exercise sequence. Finally, move the pegs so that the bar travels only a few inches during the exercise. At this peg stop, you will be capable of handling much more weight than you can from the parallel squat position.

Figure 10–3 Power rack squat

Muscles developed: quadriceps, gluteus maximus, sacrospinalis

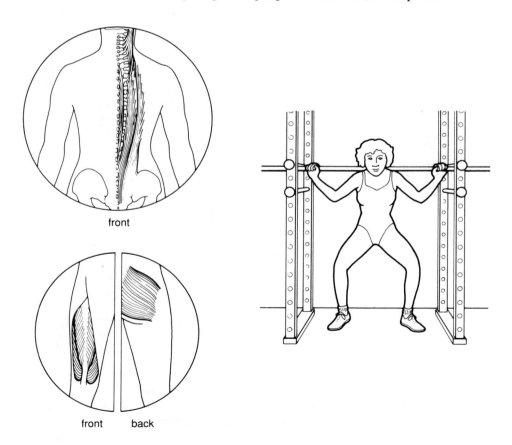

front

front   back

Leg Presses, Universal Gym and Nautilus

Leg presses are done on leg press exercise machines and can be substituted for squats. They are safer and more convenient to do than squats because they don't involve handling weight, place less stress on the back, and don't require spotters. Leg presses, however, are less effective than squats for developing strength in the quadriceps, gluteals, and hamstrings.

◆   THE TECHNIQUE   Universal Gym (Figure 10–4): Adjust the seat so that your knees are bent at a sixty- to ninety-degree angle. Grasp the side handlebars and push with your legs until your knees are fully extended. Return to the starting position. Don't bang the weights as you finish the repetition.

Figure 10–4 Leg press on Universal Gym

Muscles developed: quadriceps, gluteus maximus

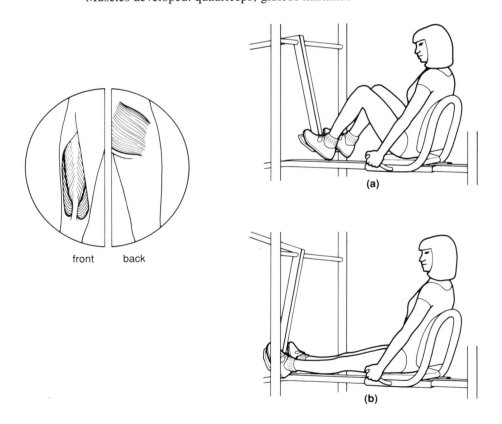

front   back

(a)

(b)

◆   THE TECHNIQUE   Nautilus Duo squat machine (Figure 10–5): Adjust the seat so that your knees are bent approximately ninety degrees. Sit with your shoulders under the shoulder pads, feet on the foot pedals, hands on the side-handles, and legs fully extended

Figure 10–5 Nautilus duo squat machine

Muscles developed: quadriceps, gluteus maximus

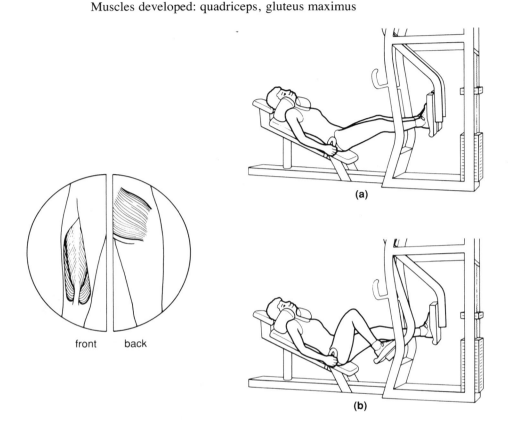

front   back

(a)

(b)

(starting position). Bend your left leg ninety degrees, then forcefully extend it. Repeat with your right leg. Then, alternate between left and right leg.

◆   THE TECHNIQUE   Nautilus leg press machine (Figure 10–6): Adjust the seat so that your knees are bent approximately ninety degrees when beginning the exercise (starting position). Push out forcefully until knees are fully extended, then return to the starting position.

Front Squats

The front squat is a variation of the squat and is used mainly in training programs of Olympic-style weight lifters. This lift isolates the leg muscles better than the regular squat, because the back cannot be used as much to assist in the movement; consequently, you cannot lift as much weight in this exercise.

Figure 10–6 Nautilus leg press machine

Muscles developed: quadriceps, gluteus maximus

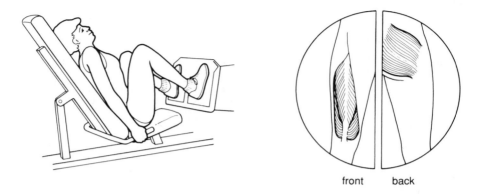

front   back

◆   THE TECHNIQUE   Standing with your feet shoulder-width apart and toes pointed
slightly outward, hold the bar on your chest, and squat down until your gluteals are one inch
below the knee (Figure 10–7). Do this exercise with good control; otherwise, you can
easily lose your balance. Stability can sometimes be improved by placing small weight
plates (five-pound plates) under your heels.

Hack Squats

Hack squats isolate the thigh muscles better than regular squats because they force you to
keep your back straighter — even more so than doing front squats. This exercise is generally
used as an auxiliary to squats rather than as the primary leg exercise.

◆   THE TECHNIQUE   In a standing position, hold a barbell behind you with arms
fully extended so that the weight rests on the back of your thighs (Figure 10–8). Slowly
squat until the weight nearly reaches the ground, then push up to the starting position.

Lunges

Lunges are a great exercise for the quadriceps (front of the thigh), gluteus maximus (buttocks), and, to a lesser extent, the calf and lower back muscles.

◆   THE TECHNIQUE   Stand with your feet shoulder-width apart and the bar resting on
the back of your shoulders, with your hands holding the bar in that position (Figure 10–9).
Lunge forward with one leg, bending it until the thigh is parallel to the floor. Repeat the
exercise using the other leg. Keep your back and head as straight as possible, and maintain
control while performing the exercise.

Figure 10–7 Front squats

Muscles developed: quadriceps, gluteus maximus, sacrospinalis, deltoid (support)

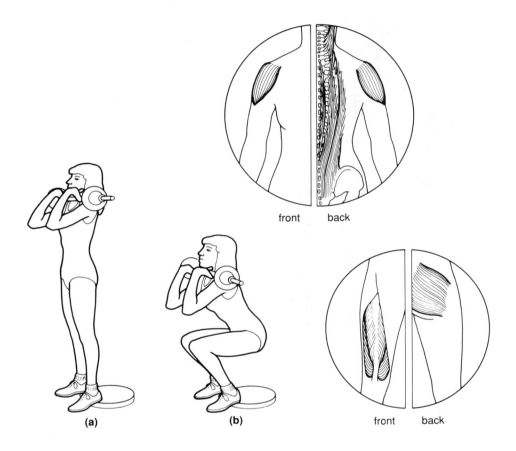

Isokinetic Squat Machines

The high-speed squat machine is a relatively new product. It is designed to add resistance when you are moving quickly during the exercise. It presents a tremendous risk of injury and has no place in the weight room.

CAUTION   ◆   Sudden loading of the spine at high speeds may cause severe damage to the intervertebral disks. High-speed squat machines are not recommended.

Figure 10–8 Hack squats

Muscles developed: quadriceps, gluteus maximus, sacrospinalis

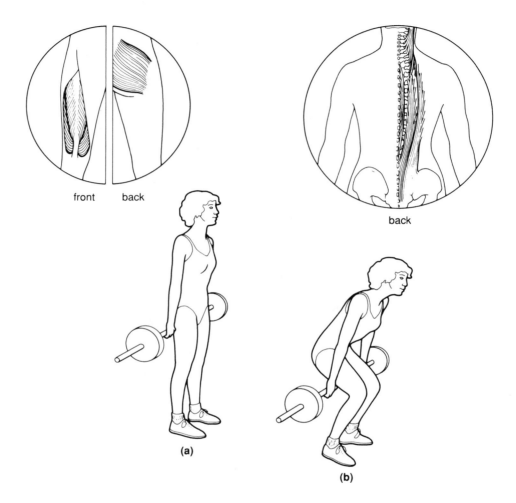

AUXILIARY EXERCISES FOR THE LOWER BODY

A number of accessory exercises for the lower body isolate distinct muscle groups, such as the quadriceps, hamstrings (back of thigh), and the muscles of the calf. Auxiliary exercises include:

- Knee extensions
- Knee flexions (leg curls)
- Heel raises

Figure 10–9 Lunges

Muscles developed: quadriceps, gluteus maximus

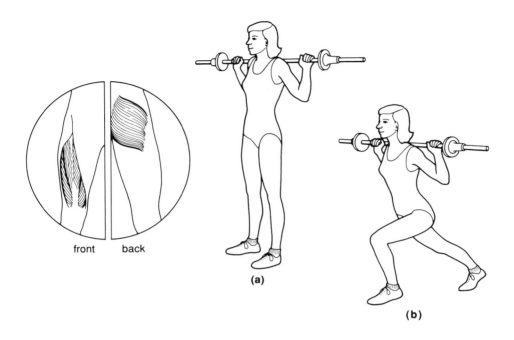

front   back

(a)

(b)

Knee Extensions

Knee extensions are done on a knee extension machine. Most gyms have these machines (Nautilus and Universal Gym both produce them). Knee extensions are excellent for building the quadriceps and are good for supplementing squats or leg presses in the general program. Doing knee extensions with weighted boots is not recommended, because it may strain the ligaments of the knee.

Knee extensions may cause kneecap pain in some women. (See the section entitled ''Kneecap Pain'' in chapter 2.) These exercises, particularly if done through a full range of motion, increase pressure on the kneecap. If you have painful kneecaps, check with an orthopedic specialist before doing this exercise.

Doing knee extensions only during the last twenty degrees of the range of motion (just before the knee is fully extended) builds up the muscle that tends to draw the kneecap toward the center of the joint. This exercise is often prescribed for women who have kneecap pain. The Lumex Company, which makes Eagle exercise equipment, makes a knee extension machine that allows you to restrict the motion done during the exercise. The Eagle knee extension machine is available in many health clubs.

Figure 10–10 Knee extensions

Muscles developed: quadriceps

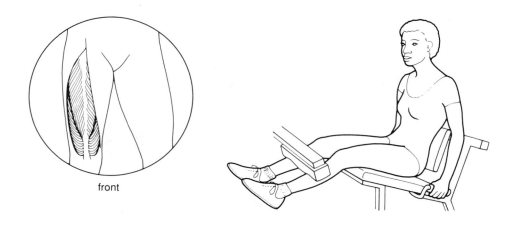

front

◆ THE TECHNIQUE Sit on the knee extension bench and place your shins on the knee extension pads (Figure 10–10). Extend your knees until they are straight, then return to the starting position.

◆ THE TECHNIQUE Universal Gym knee extension station: This exercise is done as described above. Resistance can be supplied via a cable stretching underneath the bench and connecting to a weight stack, or weights can be loaded on a peg attached to the front of the machine. (This machine is pictured in Figure 10–11.)

◆ THE TECHNIQUE Nautilus knee extension machine: The Nautilus machine is similar to those described above, except that the seat can be adjusted for differences in leg length.

Knee Flexions (Leg Curls)

Knee flexions, more commonly known as leg curls, require the use of a leg curl machine. Nautilus and Universal Gym make these machines, as do many other manufacturers. Instructions for this exercise are similar for most leg curl machines. This exercise develops the hamstrings, the muscles on the back of your thighs.

◆ THE TECHNIQUE Lie on your stomach, resting the pads of the machine just below your calf muscles (Figure 10–11). Flex your knees until they approach your buttocks, then return to the starting position. Because the hamstrings are weaker than the quadriceps, you will be unable to handle as much weight on this exercise as on the knee extension machine.

Figure 10–11 Knee flexions (leg curls)

Muscles developed: hamstrings

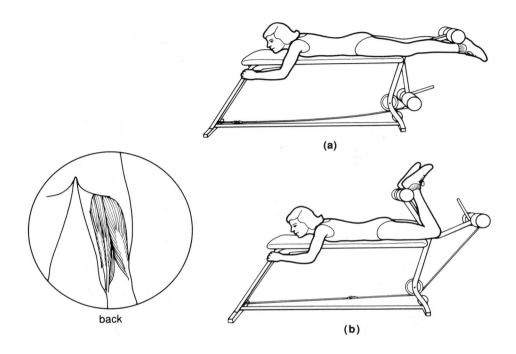

(a)

back

(b)

Most sports build the quadriceps muscles, but few work on the hamstrings. Injuries can be caused by imbalances between muscles, so it is important to work on your hamstrings in addition to your quadriceps.

Heel Raises

Heel raises strengthen the calf muscles—the soleus, gastrocnemius, and plantaris—and the Achilles tendon, which connects the calf muscles to the heel. These exercises can be done anywhere there is a step or block of wood and do not necessarily require weights.

◆   THE TECHNIQUE   Standing on the edge of a stair or block of wood with a barbell resting on your shoulders, slowly lower your heels as far as possible, then raise them until you are up on your toes (Figure 10–12). The calf muscles are very strong and require much resistance to increase their size and strength. You can add calf exercises at the end of your squat or leg press routine—do some heel raises after your last repetition.

Most gyms have some kind of calf exercise machine. Usually the machines are safer and easier to work with—you generally don't have to handle weights or worry about balance while carrying a lot of weight—and therefore are more effective than doing leg raises.

Figure 10–12 Heel raises

Muscles developed: gastrocnemius, soleus, plantaris

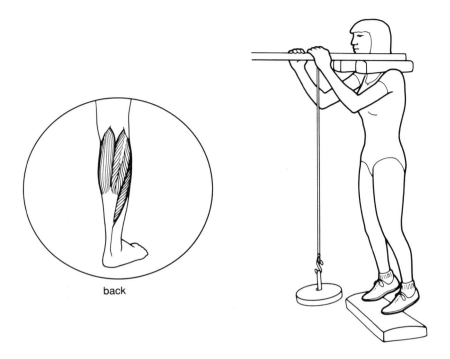

back

Heel Raises on Universal Gym

Heel raises can be conveniently done on the leg press station of the Universal Gym immediately after doing leg presses.

◆ THE TECHNIQUE   Sit in the leg extension station and fully extend your legs (starting position). Press down with your toes, then return to the starting position (Figure 10–13). You can work different portions of the calf muscles by pointing your feet straight ahead, inward, and outward.

Calf Machine (Multiexercise Machine), Nautilus

The Nautilus multiexercise machine can also be used to do pull-ups and bar dips.

◆ THE TECHNIQUE   Put the belt around your waist, attach it to the weight ring, and step up on the first step of the machine (starting position). Lift your heels and press up on your toes, then return to the starting position (Figure 10–14).

Figure 10–13 Heel raises on Universal Gym leg press station

Muscles developed: gastrocnemius, soleus, plantaris

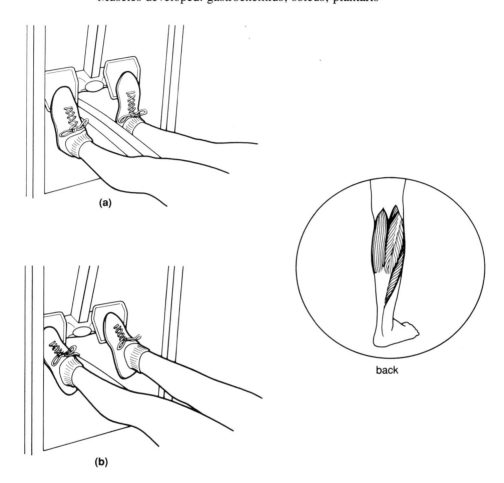

(a)

(b)

back

ADVANCED LIFTS

Popular with serious weight trainers, the advanced lifts are complex exercises that take a considerable amount of time to learn. They are valuable because they develop strength from the basic athletic position (Figure 10–1) and help improve strength and power for many sports. Basic advanced lifts include the following:

- ◆ Power cleans
- ◆ High pulls
- ◆ Dead-lifts
- ◆ Push presses

Figure 10–14 Heel raises on Nautilus multiexercise machine

Muscles developed: gastrocnemius, soleus, plantaris

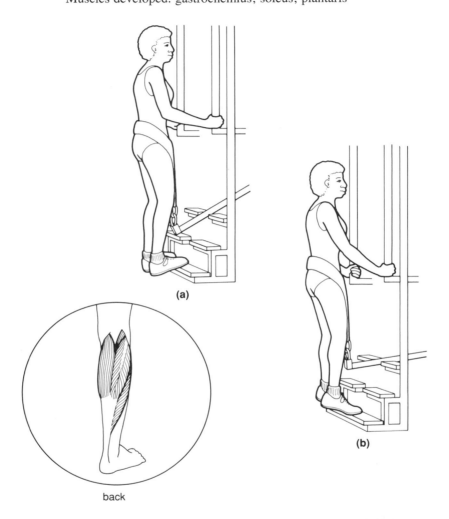

(a)

(b)

back

   These exercises should not be attempted until you have at least four to six months of weight training experience. Further, it is important that you receive instruction from a knowledgeable coach.

Power Cleans and High Pulls

The power clean is used to get the weight to the starting position for the overhead press exercise (see "Overhead Press" in chapter 6). It is an important exercise in the program of strength-speed athletes, such as throwers, heptathletes, and volleyball and basketball players.

Figure 10–15 Power cleans

Muscles developed: quadriceps, gluteus maximus, trapezius, deltoids, sacrospinalis

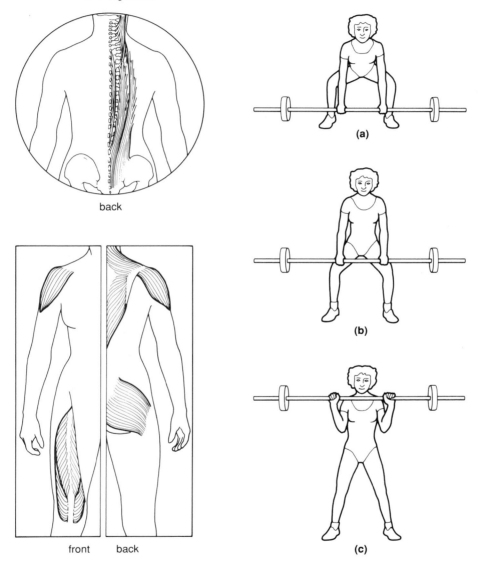

back

front   back

(a)

(b)

(c)

◆ THE TECHNIQUE   Place the bar on the floor in front of your shins (Figure 10–15). Keep your feet approximately two feet apart. Using a pronated grip, grasp the bar with your hands at shoulder-width and squat, keeping your arms and back straight and your head up. Pull the weight up past your knees to your chest while throwing your hips forward and shoulders back. The main power for this exercise should come from your hips and legs. Return the bar to the starting position.

Variations of this lift include the **high pull** (Figure 10–16), squat clean, and split clean. The high pull is identical to the power clean, except that you don't turn the bar over at the top of the lift and catch it at your chest. The high pull allows you to handle more weight and places less stress on your wrists and forearms. The squat clean and split clean, which are beyond the scope of this book, are used in Olympic weight lifting (a form of competitive weight lifting which is becoming increasingly popular with women) and take a long time to learn. The snatch (an Olympic lift) is another pulling exercise that is extremely difficult for the novice to master.

Dead Lift

The dead lift is one of the three "power lifts" (a weight lifting competition event, also becoming increasingly popular with women; the other two power lifts are the bench press

Figure 10–16 High pull

Muscles developed: quadriceps, gluteus maximus, trapezius, deltoids, sacrospinalis

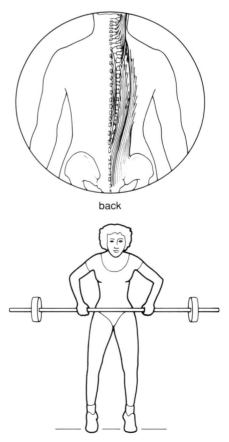

back

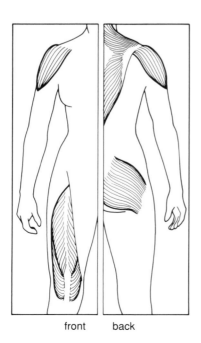

front   back

and the squat). It is an excellent exercise for the legs, buttocks, and back. Because it is possible to handle so much weight in this exercise, it is critical that proper form be maintained to avoid injury to the back.

◆   THE TECHNIQUE   Place the bar on the floor in front of your shins (Figure 10–17). Keep your feet approximately shoulder-width apart. Using a dead-lift grip (see ''Grips'' in chapter 5), grasp the bar at shoulder-width and squat down, keeping your arms and back straight and your head up. Pull the weight past your knees until you are in a fully erect position. Return the weight to the floor under control, being careful to bend only your knees and to maintain a straight back.

Figure 10–17 Dead lift

Muscles developed: quadriceps, gluteus maximus, trapezius, deltoid, sacrospinalis

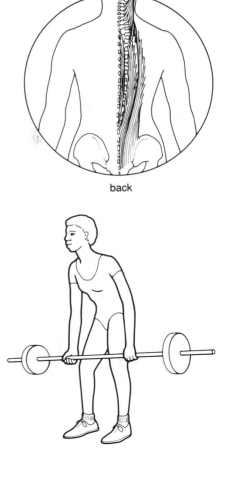

back

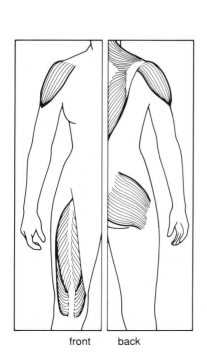

front   back

Dead lifts can also be done on the bench press station of the Universal Gym (Figure 10–18). Place a box (the kind used for step tests) in front of the bench press station. Grasp the handles with either a pronated or a dead-lift grip, with your hands shoulder-width apart. Squat down, keeping your arms and back straight and your head up. Pull the weight past your knees until you are in a fully erect position. Return to the starting position under control, without banging the weights on the weight stack and being careful to bend only your knees and to maintain a straight back.

Figure 10–18 Dead lift on Universal Gym

Muscles developed: quadriceps, gluteus maximus, trapezius, deltoid, sacrospinalis

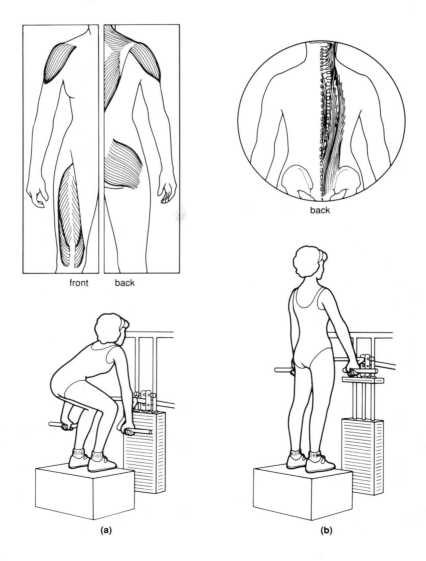

(a)   (b)

C H A P T E R

11 A Woman's Guide to Nutrition for Weight Training

NUTRITION PLAYS AN IMPORTANT ROLE IN DETERMINING THE EFFECTIVENESS OF A FITNESS and weight control program. It is extremely difficult to keep off excess body fat through exercise alone. Weight training is not a good way to burn off many calories, and unless you combine it with good nutrition and endurance exercise, you are probably doomed to failure in fighting the ''battle of the bulge.''

We are bombarded with nutritional information—some of it helpful but too much of it junk. Beware of nutritional advice that seems too good to be true. There are no nutritional supplements or drugs that will turn a weak, flabby individual into a strong and healthy person. Major changes call for hard work and dedication. Instant ''cures,'' such as mega-vitamin therapy or ''fat-burning'' pills, don't work and can be dangerous and expensive. You are better off staying with the proven principles of nutrition and participating in a steady, progressive fitness program.

Nutrition is an important factor in exercise performance. Scientists are beginning to appreciate the role of diet and nutritional manipulation in athletic success. While the balanced diet is still the cornerstone of the well-rounded fitness program, there are also various dietary techniques that have been proven effective in improving performance.

Several health issues important to women are also directly affected by nutrition and exercise. Osteoporosis (weakening of the bones), anemia, amenorrhea, and PMS are affected by nutrient intake and energy expenditure (see ''Weight Training and Your Health'' in chapter 2). Another related issue is the high rate of eating disorders among young women. It is estimated that 4–19 percent of female college students have eating problems such as bulimia, anorexia nervosa, and anorexia athletica. **Bulimia** is binge eating followed by forced vomiting. **Anorexia nervosa** is an abnormal preoccupation with weight. Women

153

with this problem tend to starve themselves and have unrealistic notions about how fat they are. **Anorexia athletica** is similar to anorexia nervosa. Besides starving themselves, women with this problem also do excessive amounts of exercise.

THE BALANCED DIET: CORNERSTONE OF THE SUCCESSFUL FITNESS PROGRAM

Billions of dollars are spent each year in the United States on diet foods and food supplements. These products include artificial sweeteners, vitamin pills, protein supplements, amino acid pills, and diet sodas. Yet it is difficult to improve upon sensible eating habits for maintaining a trim and healthy body.

The **balanced diet** plays a critical role in any fitness/nutrition program. It provides all the known nutrients, reduces the risk of **coronary artery disease**, and provides enough energy to sustain a vigorous life-style. The balanced diet consists of at least three meals a day of foods from the basic seven food groups:

◆ Milk and other dairy products (including yogurt, cottage cheese, and ice cream)

◆ Protein foods (including lean meat, fish, poultry, cheese, eggs, and beans)

◆ Fruits and vegetables (including citrus and tomatoes)

◆ Dark green and yellow vegetables

◆ Potatoes and other starchy vegetables

◆ Whole grain products (including bread and cereals)

◆ Fats (margarine and vegetable oils)

The "basic seven" food groups are an extension of the "basic four" food groups suggested by the United States Department of Agriculture in 1957. The original four food groups were (1) fruits and vegetables, (2) grains and cereals, (3) milk and milk products, and (4) high-protein foods. The basic four were extended to the basic seven to encourage people to eat fewer meat and dairy products containing cholesterol and saturated fats and more fruits, vegetables, and cereals.

The well-balanced diet satisfies the nutritional requirements established in the **Recommended Daily Allowances (RDA)** of the National Research Council of the National Academy of Sciences. The RDA are based upon present nutritional knowledge; they don't account for nutrients whose requirements have not been established. Therefore, you should consume a wide variety of foods from all the basic food groups to ensure that you take in all the nutrients your body might need. Remember, all the food supplements in the world will not make up for a poor diet.

Milk and milk products are important sources of calcium, riboflavin, high-quality protein, carbohydrates, fat, and other assorted vitamins and minerals.

Protein foods, such as meats, chicken, and fish, aside from supplying protein, also supply iron, thiamin, riboflavin, niacin, phosphorus, and zinc. Avoid eating meats with a high fat content because they are associated with increased risk of heart disease. In women, this is particularly important after the age of menopause, when the risk of heart disease rises.

The fruit and vegetable groups are important for supplying vitamins, minerals, and fiber. It is particularly important to eat dark green and deep yellow vegetables because of their high nutrient content and their possible influence in reducing the risk of certain types of cancer.

The foods in the last three categories — the starches, grains, and fats — supply thiamin, iron, niacin, and cellulose (fiber). These groups are critical for satisfying the energy requirements of a vigorous exercise program.

Fluids are a particularly important part of an active woman's diet because they directly affect exercise capacity. Body water is an essential component in most of the body's biochemical reactions and helps maintain blood volume and control body temperature. Many women avoid drinking water or fluids because they are afraid of gaining "water weight." Water is critical for health and performance. Worry about body fat instead of body weight.

A variety of effective fluid replacements have been developed that not only satisfy the body's fluid requirements but provide energy during exercise and hasten recovery after a vigorous workout. (These products will be discussed later.)

Vitamins

Incredible amounts of money are spent on **vitamin** and mineral pills every year, both by athletes and nonathletes. Among women in the United States, however, the only common documented deficiencies are iron and calcium. Therefore, with a couple of possible exceptions, anything more than a balanced diet, and maybe a "one-a-day" vitamin/mineral pill, is useless and a waste of money.

Vitamins act as co-enzymes (work with enzymes to drive the body's metabolism) and aid in the production and protection of red blood cells. Vitamins are not produced in the body and must be consumed in the diet, but they are needed in only extremely small amounts.

Of all the body's vitamins, only vitamin C, thiamin, pyridoxine, and riboflavin may be affected by exercise. Of these, only vitamin C supplementation has been shown to improve performance, and that was in adolescents who were deficient in it. Vitamin C supplementation has been a fertile area of debate since Linus Pauling suggested that megadoses of vitamin C will cure the common cold. His contention has been extremely controversial, and debate will certainly continue for many years.

There is some proof that intake of pyridoxine may decrease the symptoms of PMS. (For a discussion of PMS, see "Weight Training and Your Health" in chapter 2.) Pyridoxine is thought to increase the levels of serotonin, a hormone that elevates mood and combats depression. However, the effect of pyridoxine on PMS is controversial, and high levels of this vitamin can be toxic to the nervous system.

It appears that vitamin supplements will improve performance only if there is a nutritional deficiency. There does not appear to be any justification for the megadoses of vitamins taken by many athletes. Moreover, high doses of vitamins have been shown to cause toxic side-effects in some people. The best advice is to eat a balanced diet from the basic food groups.

Iron

Many women could benefit from iron supplementation. As many as 25–80 percent of women endurance athletes could be iron-deficient. A great deal of iron is lost through elimination (feces, urine, sweat, and menstrual blood).

Menstruating women need about eighteen milligrams (mg) of iron a day but typically only take in twelve mg per day. This can lead to a drop in iron stores in the bone marrow and, eventually, to iron-deficiency anemia (low blood count). Bone marrow is found inside many bones and is the site for red blood cell production. Iron deficiency, even without anemia, will lead to impaired performance and fatigue.

Iron found in meat, fish, and chicken is absorbed by the body much more easily than iron in other foods. So it is recommended that active women eat one of these foods or take an iron supplement every day. Some people, however, cannot tolerate iron supplements. Check with your doctor for advice about your iron needs. A simple test that measures blood ferritin can tell your doctor if you are iron-deficient.

To sum up, iron supplements are beneficial if the athlete is iron-deficient; they can have a marked effect on the body's endurance capacity and ability to transport oxygen.

Calcium

Osteoporosis, or weakening of the bones, is a common problem in women past the age of menopause. Until recently, this condition was of little interest to younger women. But it has now been established that active women who have irregular menstrual cycles have decreased bone density.

Decreased bone density in active young women is thought to be due to low levels of estrogen (a female hormone). Heavy exercise training is thought to depress estrogen production. Calcium in the diet may also be an important factor. Women with normal estrogen levels should take in at least 1,000 mg of dietary calcium per day. Those with low estrogen levels do not absorb calcium as well, so they need at least 1,500 mg per day. Dairy products — such as milk, yogurt, cottage cheese, ice cream, and hard cheese — are excellent sources of calcium. Another good source is soft-boned fish, such as salmon, trout, and sardines.

Take a calcium supplement if you can't get enough in your diet. The best calcium supplements are calcium carbonate or calcium phosphate. Beware of supplements containing bone meal and dolomite — they often contain high levels of lead, mercury, and arsenic.

Energy Requirements of Active Women

Most body functions, including the muscle contractions that allow us to lift weights and do other physical tasks, are made possible by the energy supplied by food. Carbohydrates, fats, and proteins are the three basic food components. All are essential for supplying the body's energy needs.

Active women must take in enough calories to satisfy the energy requirements of physical activity and provide the nutrients necessary for good health. Again, this can be done by consuming a well-balanced diet containing enough calories to satisfy the body's needs but not so many that you become overweight.

DEVELOPING AN ATTRACTIVE BODY: THE ROLE OF EXERCISE AND NUTRITION

The main reason for the tremendous popularity of weight training among women is that it improves physical appearance. Women who train with weights often look more athletic, tighter, and more muscular than other people. Paradoxically, some women use weight training to help them gain weight while others use it to lose weight. Is this possible? Yes, if you understand the principle of energy balance as it applies to body composition.

Weight Training, Energy Balance, and Body Composition

All the energy absorbed by the body in the form of food must be accounted for — as either energy used for body functions, energy stored as fat, or energy wasted, in the form of heat. There are no other places for food energy to go. If more energy is taken in than is needed, body fat increases. If less energy is taken in than needed, fat is lost.

It is difficult to significantly affect energy balance through weight training because it calls for few calories (compared to activities such as long-distance running). Contrary to popular belief, you cannot **spot reduce** — you cannot reduce fat in a particular area through exercise. However, weight training can have an enormous effect on appearance, even if body fat is unaltered.

Strengthening a body part, such as the abdominal muscles, increases muscle tone and "tightens up" the area. Strong muscles are less likely to sag, so the area looks more attractive. Excess fat stays — but it looks better. Weight training can play an important role in helping people gain or lose weight, or simply look more attractive, if it is practiced as part of a comprehensive diet and exercise program.

Losing Weight

Weight loss is a national obsession. Many women train with weights or do other exercises to keep their weight under control. Ultimately, the body's energy balance determines whether body fat increases, decreases, or stays the same. Fat increases when more energy is consumed than expended. While exercise is an important part of a weight control program, caloric restriction is essential if the program is to be successful.

The goal of a weight control program should be to lose body fat and maintain the loss. Quick-loss programs often lead to the loss of muscle tissue and body water. They do nothing to instill healthy long-term dietary habits that will maintain the new weight. The following principles for losing body fat will increase the chances of success for your weight control program:

◆ Stress fat loss. Rapid weight loss from fad diets is often caused by the loss of muscle mass and water. Fat loss instead of weight loss should be the goal.

◆ Restrict the weight you lose. Lose no more than one and a half or two pounds per week. More rapid weight loss results in the loss of muscle tissue.

◆ Eat a balanced diet high in complex carbohydrates and low in fat. Lose calories by combining caloric restriction with more exercise.

◆ Exercise. A critical component of a successful weight loss program is exercise, particularly endurance exercise, such as running, walking, and cycling.

◆ Monitor your body composition. Make sure that most of the weight loss is from a reduction in body fat instead of a reduction in **lean body mass**.

Gaining Weight

Many women are naturally underweight and seek to gain weight. There are two basic ways to gain weight: increasing muscle or increasing fat. Lean women can often increase fat with little or no adverse effects on appearance or health; nevertheless, they should strive to gain "quality weight." This can be done only through a vigorous weight training program that stresses the large muscle groups in the legs, hips, shoulders, arms, and chest.

Muscle weight takes many years to gain but is surely preferable to the fat that is quickly added from expensive high-calorie weight-gain supplements or unhealthy high-fat diets. Basic guidelines for gaining weight include:

◆ Stress quality over quantity (increase muscle rather than fat). Carrying extra fat does little to improve physical performance or appearance.

◆ Use weight training to increase the size of major muscle groups. Emphasize the exercises that work large muscle groups: mainly presses (e.g., bench press, seated press) and high-resistance leg exercises (e.g., squats, leg presses). For lifts, use heavy resistance and many sets (e.g., 5 sets of 5 repetitions).

◆ Concentrate on long-term gains. Do not expect to increase lean body mass by more than four to six pounds per year.

◆ Don't use drugs to gain weight. Avoid anabolic steroids and growth hormones. The benefits are not worth the risks.

◆ Eat a well-balanced diet containing slightly more calories than normal. If you are training vigorously, your protein requirement may increase slightly, from 0.8 to 1–1.5 grams per kilogram body weight.

◆ Monitor your body composition. Keep track of your progress by measuring your lean body mass and body fat. The underwater weighing technique is the most accurate. This test is done in many college and university physical education departments, sports medicine centers, and health clubs. The skin fold and electrical impedance techniques of body composition measurement are also widely available. Ask your instructor for further information.

◆ Consult a physician if you do not progress. There are a variety of explanations for being chronically underweight, including family history, maturational level, and metabolic status.

GLYCOGEN AND PERFORMANCE

Carbohydrates are the essential fuel for muscular work. They are stored in your muscles and liver as **glycogen**. Although fats and proteins are also used for energy during exercise, the need for glycogen increases with the intensity of physical activity. When your body or individual muscles are depleted of glycogen, fatigue and sluggishness set in, limiting performance.

The amount of glycogen present in the liver and muscles when exercise begins will affect endurance, capacity for intense exercise, and even mental outlook. If your muscles feel tired, you are unlikely to have a very effective workout or successful competition. Glycogen depletion causes fatigue, and if normal glycogen levels are not restored, performance levels will be impaired. The goal of an optimal athletic nutrition program is to prevent glycogen depletion during exercise and replenish glycogen stores in the muscles and liver immediately after exercise. These goals can be accomplished by eating a high-energy, high-carbohydrate diet during periods of intense training or competition and consuming carbohydrate beverages during and after training.

Preventing Glycogen Depletion

Glycogen depletion may be avoided to a certain extent if the body uses fats as fuels during exercise. This spares the muscle and liver glycogen stores. There are several ways to do this: (1) improve your ability to use fats, (2) mobilize fats early during exercise, and (3) provide alternative fuels for the muscles to slow down the use of glycogen and blood sugar.

The best way to improve your ability to use fats is through endurance training. One of the essential benefits of endurance training is that it increases the size of structures called mitochondria, which are the energy centers of the cells. This facilitates fat utilization.

The sooner you can make alternative fuels available, the sooner you can use them, sparing important carbohydrate stores. Another technique for increasing fat mobilization is ingesting caffeine. The use of carbohydrate drinks during exercise has also been shown to be effective in sparing muscle and liver glycogen and maintaining blood sugar. While caffeine ingestion before exercise and drinking carbohydrate beverages during exercise are effective in endurance exercise, their effects on strength exercises are not completely understood. Caffeine, found in coffee, soft drinks, chocolate, and tea, causes nervousness and stomach upset in some people, so it cannot be universally recommended as a means of sparing glycogen stores.

The High-Carbohydrate Diet

A high-carbohydrate diet is critical for athletes involved in heavy training. It contains the basic seven food groups but emphasizes food from the carbohydrate groups, such as cereals, fruits, and grains.

Many studies have demonstrated that this diet enables active people to exercise longer and more intensely and to recover faster than those on mixed or high-fat diets (Figure 11–1). Table 11–1 illustrates an example of a high-energy, high-carbohydrate diet, suitable for any active woman involved in intense training. This diet includes fresh vegetables for

Figure 11–1 Effect of diet on performance

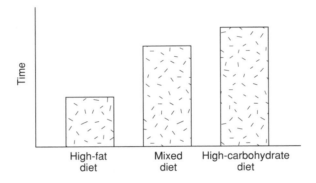

vitamins and minerals, meats and meat substitutes for protein, and avoids refined sugar products, such as cakes, pies, and candies. Alcoholic beverages should also be avoided or minimized.

Active women should take great care in designing their diets. It is important that enough calories and protein be consumed to optimize muscle growth. Too much carbohydrate in the diet will lead to fat gain. There is no one perfect diet. Experiment with a variety of foods to find a diet that's agreeable and palatable.

Carbohydrate Drinks During Exercise

A recent finding in sports medicine research has been the exciting discovery that consuming carbohydrate drinks during exercise improves performance. These drinks have been shown to enhance glycogen stores in the liver, maintain blood sugar levels, and decrease the rate of glycogen breakdown in the muscles — all of which improve exercise performance.

Just as important, the use of carbohydrate drinks following exercise results in a rapid resynthesis of glycogen. Researchers have found that the two-hour period immediately

---

TABLE 11-1
**Example of a Diet High in Energy and
Carbohydrates**

BREAKFAST

1 cup fruit juice (orange, grapefruit, guava)
Pancakes (2-3) with syrup
2 eggs (cholesterol-free egg substitutes)
Turkey sausage
Nonfat milk or hot chocolate

LUNCH

Tuna salad sandwich
Fruit
Green salad
Nonfat milk

DINNER

Pasta with meat sauce (spaghetti, lasagna, etc.)
Bread
Green salad
Fruit
Nonfat milk

---

after exercise is the best time for restoring glycogen in the muscles and liver. If you consume carbohydrate drinks during this time, you can increase glycogen levels by 20 percent.

Polylactate and **glucose polymers** are excellent fuel sources for replacing lost glycogen. These substances can be found in commercially made products, such as Cytomax (made by Champion Nutrition). Drinking a carbohydrate beverage during and immediately after exercise will allow you to come back sooner after a hard workout and possibly prevent the fatigue that accompanies low glycogen levels.

A word of caution about carbohydrate beverages: Never consume a carbohydrate drink before exercise (within one and a half hours). Carbohydrates stimulate the release of the hormone insulin. Insulin moves sugar out of the blood and into the cells, which could lead to low blood sugar during exercise. Taking a high-sugar drink before exercise will backfire and decrease performance.

Avoid High-Fat Diets

Before 1965, a breakfast of bacon, eggs, and toast, smothered in butter, was almost a tradition in the United States. Nowadays many people avoid such meals because of their high fat and cholesterol content. Studies show that diets high in fat and cholesterol increase the risk of coronary heart disease (hardening of the arteries) and some types of cancer.

Both the American Heart Association and the American Cancer Society recommend low-fat and low-cholesterol diets. So the high-carbohydrate diet that has been recommended will not only improve your physical performance, it may improve your health as well.

Protein Requirements for Weight Trainers

Protein supplements have been popular among weight trainers for many years. However, most women who train with weights don't need any more protein than the average person. The daily requirement for protein in healthy adults is about 0.8–1.0 gram of protein per kilogram of body weight. (Several recent studies suggest that athletes involved in extremely intense programs may have a higher protein requirement than average.)

Protein requirements of the human body are determined by a complicated and difficult procedure called nitrogen balance. Proteins are composed of different combinations of **amino acids**. Amino acids contain nitrogen, and the nitrogen must be eliminated to use the amino acids as fuel. Nitrogen is an important marker of protein metabolism because its elimination from the body is directly proportional to the breakdown of amino acids.

Protein breakdown in the body can be estimated by measuring nitrogen loss from the body in waste products, such as urine, feces, sweat, nail clippings, hair loss, etc. Protein intake can be estimated by measuring the quantity of nitrogen ingested in the diet. If the body is using more protein for fuel than is being taken in (a net loss of nitrogen), the person is said to be in "negative nitrogen balance." If the person is incorporating more protein into body tissues than is being expended as fuel (a net gain in nitrogen), then the body is said to be in "positive nitrogen balance."

The goal for women involved in a weight training program is to achieve a positive nitrogen balance. This means that the body is adding protein. A positive nitrogen balance suggests that the muscles are getting bigger and stronger.

Nitrogen balance studies usually show that most active women do not need more protein in their diet. The average requirement of 0.8–1.0 gram of protein per kilogram of body weight is easily satisfied by the average American diet. Extra protein is probably only necessary for elite or experienced weight-trained athletes involved in very intense training. Surely, for people training at less intense levels, protein supplements are unnecessary.

Proteins as an Energy Source

Most energy during exercise comes from carbohydrates and fats. However, proteins can also be used for energy, and they play an important role in maintaining blood sugar through a process called gluconeogenesis (the formation of new blood sugar in the liver). Maintenance of blood sugar during exercise is critical for maintaining exercise intensity. Low blood sugar causes fatigue, sluggishness, and disorientation.

Because of their effects on blood sugar and metabolic regulation, the pregame or prepractice meal should contain some protein. For many years, physicians treating people with diabetes mellitus, a disease related to faulty blood sugar regulation, have recommended a diet with a significant protein component because the amino acids are very effective in ensuring long-lasting release of sugar into the blood. In essence, the amino acids act like tiny blood-glucose-releasing capsules.

Amino Acid and Polypeptide Supplements

Amino acid and polypeptide supplements have been hailed as "natural" anabolic steroids, accelerating muscle development, decreasing body fat, and stimulating the release of growth hormones. Amino acids are the basic building blocks of proteins, and polypeptides are combinations of two or more amino acids linked together. Proponents of these supplements point to their more rapid absorption as proof of superiority over normal dietary sources of protein.

Presently, there is little scientific proof to support claims of their benefits for most active women. The protein requirement of most women who train recreationally with weights is no higher than for sedentary individuals. So the rate of amino acid absorption from the gastrointestinal track is not of any importance. For recreational weight trainers, these supplements are a waste of money.

Some indirect proof exists, however, that amino acid or polypeptide supplements may be beneficial for elite weight-trained athletes. Muscle hypertrophy (enlargement) depends on the concentration of amino acids in the muscle — the more amino acids available, the faster the rate of muscle hypertrophy. Several studies show that elite weight-trained athletes often do not consume enough protein. Also, when very large amounts of protein were consumed, the process of muscle hypertrophy was accelerated.

However, these supplements do involve risks. Consuming an unbalanced amino acid formula, one that is high in some amino acids and deficient in others, has been shown to cause negative nitrogen balance. Also, substituting amino acid or polypeptide supplements for protein-rich foods may cause deficiencies in important nutrients, such as iron and the B vitamins. Clearly amino acid supplementation is of little use to the average recreational weight trainer. So, unless you are an elite athlete, just stick to the well-balanced diet.

Other Nutritional Supplements

It is difficult to improve upon the balanced diet. However, various nutritional supplements have been studied as possible **ergogenic aids** — substances or techniques that improve performance (Table 11–2). Possible nutritional ergogenic aids recently studied include medium chain triglycerides, L-carnatine, succinates, and pyridoxine-alpha-ketoglutarate. Studies of these substances have yielded contradictory results. Some studies show that all these substances can improve performance; other studies show no effect. At this point, therefore, it is not appropriate to recommend these supplements.

ANABOLIC STEROIDS AND WOMEN

The use of anabolic steroids by women athletes is common in sports such as body building, track and field, and swimming. Athletes take anabolic steroids in the hope of gaining

TABLE 11–2
Some Techniques and Substances Used as
Ergogenic Aids

Alcohol
Amphetamines
Anabolic steroids
Aspartates
Bee pollen
Beta blockers
Caffeine
Cocaine
Cold
Digitalis
Electrical stimulation
Ephedrine
Epinephrine
Glucose
Growth hormone
Heat
Human chorionic gonadotropin
Hypnosis
Inosine
Insulin
Lactate
Marijuana
Massage
Medium chain triglycerides
Negatively ionized air
Nicotine
Nitroglycerine
Norepinephrine
Oxygen
Protein supplements
Pyridoxine-alpha-ketoglutarate
Sodium bicarbonate
Strychnine
Succinates
Sulfa drugs
Vitamins
Wheat germ oil
Yeast

TABLE 11–3
Reported Side-Effects of Anabolic Steroids

- Abnormal bleeding and blood clotting
- Acne
- Breast enlargement in males
- Decreased male hormone levels
- Depressed sperm production
- Dizziness
- Elevated blood pressure
- Elevated blood sugar
- Gastrointestinal distress
- Heart disease
- Impaired immune function
- Increased aggressiveness
- Liver cancer
- Liver toxicity
- Masculinization in women and children
- Prostatic cancer
- Stunted growth in children
- Tissue swelling

---

weight, strength, power, speed, endurance, and aggressiveness. Anabolic steroids are drugs that resemble the male hormone **testosterone**. Testosterone is important in the growth of muscle tissue as well as male primary and secondary sexual characteristics, which include development of the sex organs, facial hair, and aggressiveness.

Women, Health, and Anabolic Steroids

Many women who take anabolic steroids are not aware of the risks involved. The drugs are very effective — they will increase muscle size and strength in most women — but the side-effects are great. These potentially dangerous substances are usually taken without medical supervision, and there have been many reports of serious illness or death resulting from their use. (See Table 11–3.) Among the most serious side-effects in women are liver disease, heart disease, severe mental illness, and masculinization. The benefits are clearly not worth the health risks.

Women can expect greater gains than men from the use of anabolic steroids because the starting levels of circulating male hormones in females is low. However, the side-effects are more severe in women. Aside from masculinization, women will typically experience acne, changes in skin texture, severe fluid retention, unnatural increases in muscle mass, and radically altered cholesterol metabolism. Clitoral enlargement and menstrual irregularity are also possible. Many of these changes are irreversible.

The long-term consequences of anabolic steroid use in healthy women are not completely understood either. The effects on future fertility are unknown. The use of these drugs may lead to coronary heart disease and liver cancer. These conditions may take many years to develop. A woman who doesn't experience any side-effect from the drugs when young may be setting the stage for serious disease in later life. Generally, the severity of the side-effects seems to be affected by dosage and duration of drug therapy. Athletes taking anabolic steroids may be playing "Russian roulette."

EATING DISORDERS

Being thin and young is presented by the media as ideal for women. This has resulted in an epidemic of eating disorders in industrialized countries. Over 90 percent of all people with anorexia nervosa and bulimia are women.

Men are not immune from such compulsive behavior, but they display it differently than women. Men who exercise to excess, even when severely injured, are called "obligatory runners." These men run more than fifty miles a week. When they can't exercise, they become extremely depressed. The common denominator in these conditions is an over-emphasis on achievement and acceptance by others.

Anorexia Nervosa and Anorexia Athletica

These eating disorders are closely related. Anorexia nervosa is an obsessive preoccupation with and fear of gaining weight. The person uses extreme diets and becomes focused on becoming thin at the expense of other goals. Anorexia athletica is a variation of anorexia nervosa. Besides severe dieting, the person overdoes exercise.

Typically, the person with anorexia is a young woman of high school or college age. She is seen by parents and friends as exceedingly conscientious, with an overly organized life. She usually has low self-esteem and an extreme wish to please others. She may have somewhat of a weight problem. Sometimes anorexia may develop because of depression, illness, or peer pressure.

Women often report experiencing a type of "high" when they first use their punishing diet routine. Researchers speculate that this may be a result of the increased attention they get from losing weight. It has also been suggested that the "high" comes from the body's releasing of hormones called endorphins to combat the intense feelings of hunger accompanying the diet. Endorphins produce an effect similar to opium and are one of the body's ways of dealing with pain.

As the condition develops, the person uses an increasingly strict diet and does more exercise. Physical symptoms common to women with anorexia include extreme weight loss, dry skin, loss of hair, brittle finger nails, cold hands and feet, low blood pressure and heart rate, swelling around the ankles and hands, and weakening of the bones.

Anorexia nervosa is characterized by the following disorders:

◆ Extreme weight loss. A woman with anorexia typically loses at least 25 percent of her original weight. With the weight loss, she often experiences insomnia (inability to sleep) and a decreased ability to tolerate cold. She may wear many layers of clothes to keep her warm and hide her extreme weight loss.

◆ Unrealistic body image. She sees herself as overweight, even when others describe her as painfully thin. This distorted image gets worse as she loses weight.

◆ Extreme diets. She generally restricts her food intake for extended periods, even when extremely hungry. She will usually try to eliminate carbohydrates from the diet and often becomes a vegetarian.

◆ Obsession with food. She will often daydream about food, able to think of nothing else. She may become involved in preparing elaborate meals for others as part of her obsession.

   She also has a great fear of losing control and gaining back all the weight she has lost. She lives by the notion that she can't lose enough weight and still has a long way to go.

◆ Drug use. She may abuse drugs, particularly stimulants, such as amphetamines, which depress appetite. She may also use emetics to help her vomit, diuretics to lose water weight, and laxatives to clear out her digestive tract. (The excessive use of laxatives leads to constipation in people with anorexia.)

◆ Amenorrhea. It is likely that she will stop having periods. This will happen early in the condition, even before much weight is lost.

◆ Excessive exercise. She uses exercise as a way of losing more weight. She often runs herself to exhaustion and extreme weakness.

◆ Depression. The woman with anorexia probably feels extremely depressed. She has very low self-esteem, decreased sex drive, feelings of hopelessness, and sometimes suicidal thoughts.

Bulimia

A woman with bulimia will go on an eating binge and consume thousands of calories. Usually, but not always, she induces vomiting afterward. People with bulimia are often also anorexic, but not necessarily. After the eating binge, the person is typically very depressed and ashamed. She usually resolves to go on a strict diet. This leads to a vicious cycle of binge eating and dieting.

Women with bulimia will usually suffer from decayed teeth, enlarged salivary glands, dehydration, abnormally low blood levels of potassium and chloride, and abnormal heart rhythms and brain waves.

Treating Eating Disorders

Because eating disorders are so common among young women, you should be aware of their warning signs and risk factors. The physical signs — excessive weight loss, low blood pressure, obsessive behavior, dry skin, cold hands and feet — have been discussed. Young women who are slightly overweight and have low self-esteem are at greatest risk. The best thing you can do is recognize you have the problem early. Treatments are not very effective for women who have had these eating disorders for a long time.

Treatment should fit the severity of the problem. You could have one or two physical symptoms typical of anorexia without actually having the condition. Perhaps you just need to learn about good eating habits. You should get a checkup, too. If there is any possibility that you have an eating disorder, however, seek psychological counseling and medical help right away.

Medical treatment includes hospitalization to stabilize serious cases, medications to treat depression, and behavior modification to change your eating habits. Anorexia and bulimia can cause serious health problems and even death. They should not be taken lightly.

Certain social and psychological factors increase the risk of developing these disorders:

◆ The belief that the only way to be beautiful and happy is to be thin

◆ Family history of eating disorders

◆ Lack of emotional support from your family

◆ Overemphasis on achievement

◆ Rigid, overprotective parents

If you have any risk factors or overt symptoms of eating disorders, seek help before you have a real problem on your hands. See your physician or counselor about your problem. You don't have to commit to long-term treatment. A meeting may help you understand if you have a problem or just the normal, temporary setbacks of living.

Muscular System

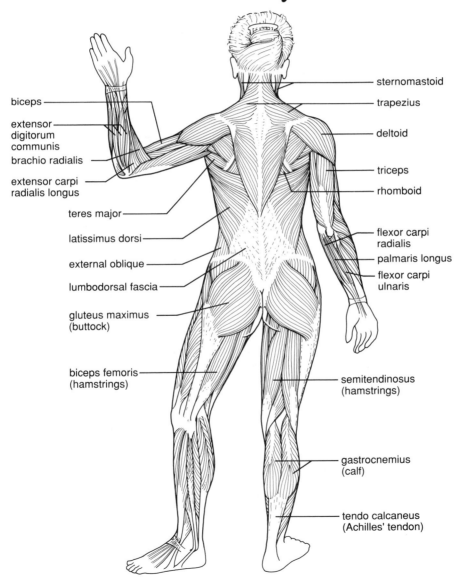

biceps

extensor digitorum communis

brachio radialis

extensor carpi radialis longus

teres major

latissimus dorsi

external oblique

lumbodorsal fascia

gluteus maximus (buttock)

biceps femoris (hamstrings)

sternomastoid

trapezius

deltoid

triceps

rhomboid

flexor carpi radialis

palmaris longus

flexor carpi ulnaris

semitendinosus (hamstrings)

gastrocnemius (calf)

tendo calcaneus (Achilles' tendon)

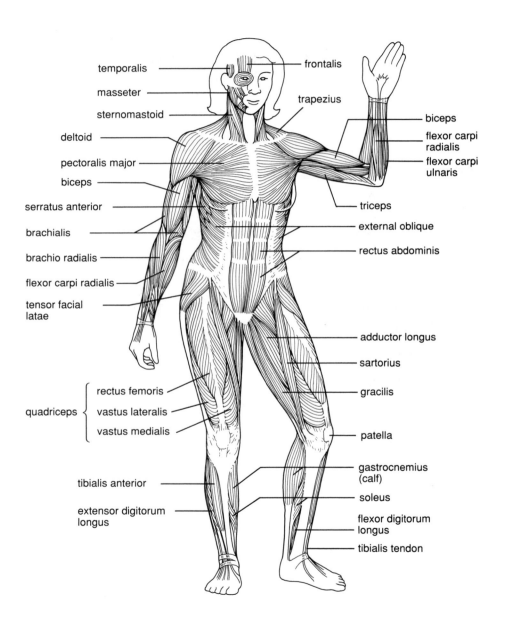

temporalis

masseter

sternomastoid

deltoid

pectoralis major

biceps

serratus anterior

brachialis

brachio radialis

flexor carpi radialis

tensor facial
latae

quadriceps {
rectus femoris

vastus lateralis

vastus medialis

tibialis anterior

extensor digitorum
longus

frontalis

trapezius

biceps

flexor carpi
radialis

flexor carpi
ulnaris

triceps

external oblique

rectus abdominis

adductor longus

sartorius

gracilis

patella

gastrocnemius
(calf)

soleus

flexor digitorum
longus

tibialis tendon

APPENDIX 2

Sample Weight Programs to Build Strength for Sports

GENERAL PROGRAM

◆ Train with weights three days per week (no less than two).

◆ Participate in aerobic (endurance) exercise three to five days per week. Good aerobic exercises include walking, jogging, swimming, and cycling. Start-and-stop sports such as tennis, racquetball, and basketball are acceptable if the intensity of play is vigorous.

◆ Do flexibility (stretching) exercises for your major muscle groups at least five days per week. All stretching should be done statically (don't bounce). Stretch the muscle until you feel tightness without pain. Hold the stretch for fifteen to sixty seconds.

Example of General Weight Training Program

EXERCISE	SETS	REPETITIONS
Bench press	3	10
Lat pulls	3	10
Lateral raises	3	10
Biceps curls	3	10
Triceps extensions	3	10
Abdominal curls	3	10
Squats	3	10
Calf raises	3	10

CONDITIONING FOR ALPINE SKIING

◆ Participate in aerobic exercise three to five times per week. Running, cross-country skiing, and cycling are probably the best forms of endurance exercise for alpine skiers. Include some high intensity aerobics (fast running, fast cycling, and so on) in your program because skiing often requires rapid, powerful movements.

◆ Although total body conditioning is critical, concentrate on lower body exercises in the weight training program. In addition to leg exercises, do exercises for the back, abdominals, and shoulders.

◆ Stretch every day. Flexibility is extremely important for preventing injury and achieving optimal technique.

Sample Program for Alpine Skiers

EXERCISE	SETS	REPETITIONS
Lat pulls	3	10
Bench press	3	10
Triceps push-downs	3	10
Abdominal curls	3	25
Back extensions	3	15
Knee extensions	3	10
Knee flexions	3	10
Squats	3	10
Calf raises	3	10

CONDITIONING FOR TENNIS

◆ Tennis is largely an anaerobic activity (start-and-stop), but endurance is important and an adjunct running program is helpful for achieving optimal fitness for the sport. Try to run at least two days a week (in addition to playing tennis). Run fast at least one day a week. An example of a fast running workout is to sprint or stride the straightaways of a 400-meter running track and walk the turns. On the other running days, jog two to five miles.

◆ Stretch at least five days a week. Important areas to stretch are the shoulders, thighs, hamstrings, and forearm extensor muscles.

◆ Weight training should stress general conditioning but should also include exercises for the rotator cuff muscles of the shoulder and forearm extensor muscles. These additional exercises will help prevent injuries to the shoulder and elbow, which are extremely common in tennis players.

Sample Program for Tennis Players

EXERCISE	SETS	REPETITIONS
Bench press	3	10
Lat pulls	3	10
Biceps curls	3	10
Triceps extensions	3	10
Abdominal curls	3	10
Squats	3	10
Calf raises	3	10
Rotator cuff exercises	3	10
Empty can exercise	3	10
Wrist extensions	3	10

CONDITIONING FOR VOLLEYBALL

◆ Like tennis, volleyball is a start-and-stop activity requiring quickness, explosiveness, and endurance. Run at least two days a week to supplement endurance fitness. One of those days should include fast running and sprinting.

◆ Plyometric exercises (see chapter 4) are helpful for improving your ability to jump. Do not do excessive amounts of plyometrics until you are well conditioned. Try to perform leg exercises explosively. This will improve the height of your jumps.

◆ Stretch regularly to help prevent injuries.

◆ Upper and lower body exercises are important for volleyball players. In addition to major muscle exercises for the legs and upper body, include exercises for the calves, rotator cuffs (shoulders), and back.

Sample Program for Volleyball Players

EXERCISE	SETS	REPETITIONS
Bench press	3	10
Push-presses or jerks	3	10
Lat pulls	3	10
Biceps curls	3	10
Triceps extensions	3	10
Abdominal curls	3	10
Squats	3	10
Calf raises	3	10
Rotator cuff exercises	3	10
Empty can exercise	3	10

CONDITIONING FOR SOFTBALL .

◆ Softball requires powerful legs and hips because the muscle groups in these areas supply the power to hit the ball. Work on muscle groups susceptible to injury such as the rotator cuff (shoulder), hamstrings, quadriceps, and lower back.

◆ Do stretching exercises for the quadriceps, hamstrings, shoulders, and lower back.

◆ Run at least three days per week. During the off-season, begin with jogging, then progress to sprints.

Weight Training for Softball

EXERCISE	SETS	REPETITIONS
Bench press	3	10
Lat pulls	3	10
Biceps curls	3	10
Hamstring curls	3	10
Triceps extensions	3	10
Abdominal curls	3	10
Squats	3	10
Calf raises	3	10
Rotator cuff exercises	3	10
Empty can exercise	3	10
Wrist extensions/flexions	3	10
Back extensions	3	10

CONDITIONING FOR GOLF

◆ Golf requires lower body explosiveness, flexibility in the torso, and strong arms and shoulders.

◆ While golf does not require a high degree of aerobic fitness, it is important to be able to walk long distances without tiring. Walking is perhaps the best physical preparation for the sport. Try to walk at least three days a week for forty-five to sixty minutes.

◆ Injuries to the back are relatively common among golfers. It is important to develop good strength and flexibility in the lower back. Work on flexibility of the back, hips, and shoulders every day.

Weight Training for Golfers

EXERCISE	SETS	REPETITIONS
Bench press	3	10
Lat pulls	3	10
Biceps curls	3	10
Triceps extensions	3	10
Abdominal curls	3	10
Twists	3	20
Squats	3	10
Wrist extensions/flexions	3	10
Back extensions	3	10
Isometric back exercise	3	10

Glossary

Adaptation: Changes in the body as a result of a biological stressor. For example, forcing muscles to contract against increased resistance causes them to increase in size.

Aerobics: Exercises that increase oxygen consumption, such as running or swimming, and improve respiratory and circulatory function.

Amenorrhea: Absence of menstruation.

American College of Sports Medicine: The principal interdisciplinary organization of sports medicine professionals. Represented disciplines include medicine, athletic training, exercise physiology, physical therapy, psychology, motor learning (study of how physical skills are learned), biomechanics (study of motion), chiropractic, and education.

Amino acids: Substances that form the principal components of proteins. They are taken in supplement form by some people to enhance muscle growth, but there is no evidence that they are effective.

Anabolic steroids: Synthetic male hormones taken by people to enhance athletic performance and body composition. (Anabolic biochemical building processes.)

Androgens: Hormones that promote male sexual characteristics and cell protein synthesis. They are produced in the male testes and in the adrenal glands of both sexes.

Anorexia athletica: An eating disorder related to anorexia nervosa. People with this condition include excessive exercise as part of their obsessive preoccupation with body weight.

Anorexia nervosa: An eating disorder characterized by a neurotic fixation on body fat and food.

Atrophy: Decrease in size of a body part or tissue.

Balanced diet: A diet composed of the basic food groups: dairy products, cereals and grains, fruits and vegetables, and meat and high-protein foods.

Body building: A form of weight training dedicated to improving the shape and appearance of the body.

Bulimia: An eating disorder characterized by binge eating followed by forced vomiting.

Carbohydrate: Organic compounds, such as sugars and starches, composed of carbon, hydrogen, and oxygen.

Carbohydrate loading: A diet and nutritional technique that results in an unusual concentration of glycogen in the liver and skeletal muscle.

Circuit training: A technique involving a series of weight training stations. The weight trainer performs an exercise and rapidly moves to the next station with little or no rest. Circuit training develops cardiovascular endurance, though not as effectively as endurance exercises such as running, cycling, or swimming.

Collar: Device that secures weights to barbells or dumbbells.

Concentric muscle contraction: Application of force as the muscle shortens.

Constant resistance: A form of weight training that uses a constant load, such as a barbell or dumbbell.

Cool-down: A light exercise program done at the end of a workout to gradually return the body to its normal resting state.

Coronary heart disease: A disease of the large arteries supplying the heart, sometimes called hardening of the arteries.

Cycle training: A training technique that varies the type, volume, rest intervals, and intensity of workouts throughout the year. Also called ''periodization of training.''

Dead-lift grip: Gripping the bar with one palm toward you and one away; sometimes called ''mixed grip.''

Dysmenorrhea: Painful menstruation.

Eccentric loading: Loading the muscle while it is lengthening; sometimes called ''negatives.''

Eccentric muscle contraction: Application of force as the muscle lengthens.

Electrical muscle stimulation: Application of an electrical current to the skin over a muscle group for the purpose of contracting the muscle.

Endurance: The ability to sustain a specific exercise intensity.

Ergogenic aid: A substance or technique used to improve performance.

Exercise physiology: The study of physiological function during exercise.

Failure method: Doing an exercise to the point of fatigue.

Glucose polymers: A group of glucose (sugar) molecules that have been chemically linked together, used as an energy component in athletic fluid replacement beverages.

Glycogen: A complex carbohydrate stored principally in the liver and skeletal muscle. It is an extremely important fuel during most forms of exercise.

Hyperplasia: Increase in the number of muscle cells (fibers).

Hypertrophy:　Increase in the size of a muscle fiber. Hypertrophy is usually stimulated by muscular overload.

Incontinence:　Involuntary urine leakage.

Intensity:　The relative effort expended during an exercise; also, the amount of resistance or weight used.

Interval training:　Repeated bouts of exercise that manipulate speed, distance, repetition, and rest interval. Typically used to provide an intensity overload.

Isokinetic:　Application of force at a constant speed. A form of isotonic exercise.

Isometric:　Application of force without movement. Also called "static."

Isotonic:　Application of force resulting in movement. Also called "dynamic."

Joint:　Places where bones intersect. Joints are often surrounded by joint capsules and are supported by ligaments and, to a lesser degree, by muscles.

Kegel exercise:　Exercise that involves contracting the muscles that control urine flow. This strengthens the pelvic floor muscles that support the uterus, vagina, and other lower abdominal organs.

Lean body mass:　Fat-free body weight.

Ligaments:　Structures that connect bone to bone.

Load:　The intensity of exercise, i.e., the weight or resistance used.

Maximum lift:　The maximum amount of weight you can lift in one repetition of an exercise.

Motor unit:　A motor nerve (nerve that initiates movement) connected to one or more muscle fibers.

Motor unit recruitment:　Activation of motor units by the central nervous system to exert force.

Multipennate muscle:　A muscle in which the fibers are aligned in several directions.

Oligomenorrhea:　Irregular menstruation.

Osteoporosis:　A disease characterized by bone demineralization that is most common in postmenopausal women.

Overload:　To subject the body to more than normal stress.

Overtraining:　A condition caused by training too much or too intensely and not providing enough time to recover adequately. Symptoms include lack of energy, decreased physical performance, fatigue, depression, aching muscles and joints, and proneness to injury.

Pelvis (cavity):　The canal within the skeletal pelvis that contains the bladder, rectum, pelvic colon, and some reproductive organs.

Periodization of training:　A training technique that varies the volume and intensity of exercises between workouts. Also called "cycle training."

Plyometrics:　Rapid stretching of a muscle group that is undergoing eccentric stress (i.e., the muscle is exerting force while it lengthens) followed by a rapid concentric contraction. Sometimes called "implosion training."

Polylactate: A group of lactate molecules that have been chemically linked together, used as an energy component in athletic fluid replacement beverages.

Power: In physics, power equals work per unit of time. In weight training, power is usually defined as the ability to exert force rapidly.

Power rack: A device used to restrict the range of motion during an exercise.

Premenstrual syndrome (PMS): A condition that typically occurs during the last five days before the menstrual period, often characterized by extreme anxiety, depression, mood swings, headaches, and water retention.

Pronated grip: Gripping the bar with palms away from you.

Prostaglandins: Substances released by cells that can cause changes in blood flow, fluid balances, and muscle contraction, resulting in dysmenorrhea.

Pyramiding: A training technique that uses increasing amounts of weight with succeeding sets. After a maximum weight is reached, the remaining sets are done with decreasing amounts of weight.

Rack: A structure that holds or supports barbells. Racks are often used in squats, bench presses, incline presses, and preacher curls.

Recommended Daily Allowances (RDA): Minimum nutrient requirements. Recommendations are made by the National Research Council of the National Academy of Sciences.

Rehabilitation: The restoration of normal function through the use of therapeutic exercise and modalities.

Repetition: The number of times an exercise is done during one set.

Resistance: A measure of force that must be exerted by the muscles to perform an exercise.

Rest: The period of time in between exercises, sets of exercises, or workouts.

Reversibility: Decrease in fitness caused by lack of training or injury.

RM: Repetition maximum. How much weight you can lift for a certain number of repetitions. For example, 1-RM is the amount of weight you can lift for one repetition.

Set: A group of repetitions followed by rest.

Specificity of training: Training the body so that it adapts in a particular way.

Speed loading: Moving a load as rapidly as possible.

Sports medicine: A branch of medicine dealing with medical problems of athletes. Disciplines often considered part of sports medicine include exercise physiology, athletic training, biomechanics (study of motion), sports physical therapy, kinesiology, sports psychology, motor learning (study of how physical skills are learned), and sports chiropractic.

Spot: To assist with an exercise. The spotter's main job is to help the lifter with the weight if the exercise can't be completed.

Spot reducing: Reducing fat in a specific part of the body, such as the abdomen, legs, or hips. There is no evidence that spot reducing is possible. Except for plastic surgery (liposuction), it appears that body fat can only be lost by inducing a negative energy balance — expending more energy than you take in.

Strength: The ability to exert force.

Strength-speed sport: A sport that requires rapid, powerful movements. Examples include softball, soccer, tennis, alpine skiing, and field hockey.

Stress: In weight training, stress is the resistance placed on muscles and joints during an exercise.

Super sets: Two sets of exercises performed in rapid succession, usually working opposing muscle groups.

Supinated grip: Gripping the bar with palms toward you.

Tendons: Rigid structures that connect muscles to bones.

Testosterone: The principal male hormone (androgen). It is produced by the testes, is responsible for the development of secondary sexual characteristics, and plays a role in muscle hypertrophy. (The principal androgen in women is androstenedione, produced by the adrenal glands.)

Variable resistance: The imposition of variable loading during an exercise. Resistance is generally increased toward the end of the range of motion. Usually, you must use weight machines to do variable resistance exercises.

Vitamins: A general term used to describe a group of organic substances, required in small amounts, that are essential to metabolism.

Volume: The number of sets and repetitions in a workout.

Warm-up: Low-intensity exercise done before full-effort physical activity in order to improve muscle and joint performance, prevent injury, reinforce motor skills, and maximize blood flow to the muscles and heart. In weight training, people often warm up by lifting lighter weights before attempting heavy weights.

Weight lifting belt: A belt, approximately four inches wide, used to support the abdomen and back and maintain proper spinal alignment during weight lifting exercises.

Wraps: Joint supports made of elastic bandages, neoprene, or leather.

References

Ahlborg, G., and P. Felig. 1976. "Influence of glucose ingestion on fuel-hormone response during prolonged exercise." *J. Appl. Physiol.* 41:683–88.

American Association for Health, Physical Education, and Recreation. 1971. *Nutrition for the Athlete*. Washington, D.C.: AAHPER.

Belko, A. Z. "Vitamins and exercise — an update." 1987. *Med. Sci. Sports Exerc.* 19 (Supp.): 191–96.

Bergstrom, J., L. Hermansen, E. Hultman, and B. Saltin. 1967. "Diet, muscle glycogen and physical performance." *Acta Physiol. Scand.* 71:140–50.

Brooks, G. A. 1987. "Amino acid and protein metabolism during exercise and recovery." *Med. Sci. Sports Exerc.* 19 (Supp.): 150–56.

Brooks, G. A., and T. D. Fahey. 1984. *Exercise Physiology: Human Bioenergetics and Its Applications*. New York: Macmillan.

Brooks, G. A., and T. D. Fahey. 1987. *Fundamentals of Human Performance*. New York: Macmillan.

Brown, R. D., and J. M. Harrison. 1986. "The effects of a strength training program on the strength and self-concept of two female age groups." *Res. Quart. Sport. Exerc.* 57: 315–20.

Buskirk, E. R. 1977. "Diet and athletic performance." *Postgrad. Med.* 61:229–36.

Buskirk, E. R. 1981. "Some nutritional considerations in the conditioning of athletes." *Ann. Rev. Nutr.* 1:319–50.

Butterfield, G., and D. Calloway. 1984. "Physical activity improves protein utilization in young men." *Br. J. Nutr.* 51:171–84.

Buzina, K., R. Buzina, G. Brubacker, J. Sapunar, and S. Christeller. 1984. "Vitamin C status and physical working capacity in adolescents." *In. J. Vit. Nutr. Res.* 54: 55–60.

Celejowa, I., and M. Homa. 1970. "Food intake, nitrogen and energy balance in Polish weight lifters, during a training camp." *Nutrition and Metabolism* 12:259–74.

Consolazio, C. F., H. L. Johnson, R. A. Dramise, and J. A. Skata. 1975. "Protein metabolism during intensive physical training in the young adult." *Am. J. Clin. Nutr.* 28:29–35.

Costill, D. L., A. Bennett, G. Brahnam, and D. Eddy. 1973. "Glucose ingestion at rest and during prolonged severe exercise." *J. Appl. Physiol.* 34:764–69.

Costill, D. L., and J. M. Miller. 1980. "Nutrition for endurance sport: Carbohydrate and fluid balance." *Int. J. Sports Med.* 1:2–14.

Cubric, M., and H. J. Appell. 1987. "Effect of electrical stimulation of high and low frequency on maximum isometric force and some morphological characteristics in men." *Int. J. Sports Med.* 8:256–60.

Darden, E. 1984. *The Nautilus Advanced Body Building Book*. New York: Simon & Schuster, Inc.

Darden, E. 1982. *The Nautilus Bodybuilding Book*. Chicago: Contemporary Books, Inc.

DeLorme, R., and F. Stransky. 1990. *Fitness and Fallacies*. Dubuque, Iowa: Kendall/Hunt Publishing Co.

Dohm, G. L., G. J. Kasperek, E. B. Tappscott, and E. B. Beecher. 1980. "Effect of exercise on synthesis and degradation of muscle protein." *Biochem. J.* 188:255–62.

Dragan, G. I. A., A. Vasiliu, and E. Georgescu. 1985. "Effect of increased supply of protein on elite weight-lifters." In *Milk Proteins*, ed. T. E. Galesloot and B. J. Tinbergen, 99–103. Wageningen, The Netherlands: Prodoc.

Duff, R. W., and L. K. Hong. 1984. "Self images of women bodybuilders." *Soc. Sport J.* 1:374–80.

Enoka, R. M. 1988. "Muscle strength and its development." *Sports Medicine* 6:146–68.

Fahey, T. D. 1987. *Athletic Training: Principles and Practice*. Mt. View, Calif.: Mayfield Publishing Co.

Fahey, T. D. 1989. *Basic Weight Training*. Mt. View, Calif.: Mayfield Publishing Co.

Foster, C., D. L. Costill, and W. J. Fink. 1979. "Effects of preexercise feedings on endurance performance." *Med. Sci. Sports* 11:1–5.

Gollnick, P. D., K. Piehl, I. V. Saubert, C. W. Armstrong, and B. Saltin. 1972. "Diet, exercise, and glycogen changes in human muscle fibers." *J. Appl. Physiol.* 33:421–25.

Gontzea, I., R. Sutzescu, and S. Dumitrache. 1975. "The influence of adaptation to physical effort on nitrogen balance in man." *Nutr. Rep. Int.* 11:231–36.

Gonyea, W. J., and D. Sale. 1982. "Physiology of weight lifting." *Arch. Phys. Med. Rehabil.* 63:235–37.

Haskell, W., J. Scala, and J. Whittam, eds. 1982. *Nutrition and Athletic Performance*. Palo Alto: Bull Publishing.

Haymes, E. M. 1987. "Nutritional concerns: Needs for iron." *Med. Sci. Sports Exerc.* 19 (Supp.): 197–200.

Hecker, A. L. 1982. "Nutritional conditioning and athletic performance." *Primary Care* 9:545–56.

Holloway, J., A. Beuter, and J. L. Duda. 1988. "Self efficacy and training for strength in adolescent girls." *J. Appl. Sport Psych.* 18:699–719.

Hultman, E. 1967. "Muscle glycogen in man determined in needle biopsy specimens: Method and normal values." *Scand. J. Clin. Lab. Invest.* 19:209–17.

Ikai, M., and T. Fukunaga. 1968. "Calculation of muscle strength per unit cross-sectional area of human muscle by means of ultrasonic measurement." *Int. Z. angew. Physiol. einschl. Arbeitsphysiol.* 26:26–32.

Jansson, E. 1980. "Diet and muscle metabolism in man." *Acta Physiol. Scand.* (Supp.) 487:1–24.

Jette, M., O. Pelletier, L. Parker, and J. Thoden. 1978. "The nutritional and metabolic effects of a carbohydrate-rich diet in a glycogen supracompensation training regimen." *Am. J. Clin. Nutr.* 31:2140–48.

Karlsson, J., and B. Saltin. 1971. "Diet, muscle glycogen and endurance performance." *J. Appl. Physiol.* 31:203–6.

Kasperek, G. J., and R. D. Snider. 1985. "Increased protein degradation after eccentric exercise." *Eur. J. Appl. Physiol.* 54:30–34.

Katch, F., and W. D. McArdle. 1977. *Nutrition, Weight Control, and Exercise.* Boston: Houghton Mifflin Co.

Kleiber, M. 1961. *The Fire of Life.* New York: Wiley & Sons.

Komi, P. V. 1988. "The musculoskeletal system." In A. Dirix, H. G. Knuttgen, and K. Tittel, eds., *The Olympic Book of Sports Medicine*, 15–39. London: Blackwell Scientific Publications.

Komi, P. V. 1986. "Training of muscle strength and power: Interaction of neuromotoric, hypertrophic, and mechanical factors." *Int. J. Sports Med.* 7:10–15.

Krause, M. V., and L. K. Mahan. 1979. *Food, Nutrition, and Diet Therapy.* Philadelphia: W. B. Saunders.

Lamb, D. R. 1987. "Anabolic steroids in athletics: How well do they work and how dangerous are they?" *Amer. J. Sports Med.* 12:31–38.

Lemon, P. W. R. 1987. "Protein and exercise: Update 1987." *Med. Sci. Sports Exerc.* 19 (Supp.):179–90.

Maughan, R. J., J. S. Watson, and J. Weir. 1983. "Relationship between muscle strength and muscle cross-sectional area in male sprinters and endurance runners." *Eur. J. Appl. Physiol.* 50:309–18.

Mayer, J., and B. Bullin. 1974. "Nutrition, weight control and exercise." In W. Johnson and E. R. Buskirk, eds., *Science and Medicine of Exercise and Sport.* New York: Harper and Row.

Morgan, W., ed. 1972. *Ergogenic Aids and Muscular Performance.* New York: Academic Press.

Moritani, T., and H. A. deVries. 1979. "Neural factors versus hypertrophy in the time course of muscle strength gain." *Amer. J. Phys. Med.* 58:115–30.

Morton, M. J., M. S. Paul, and J. Metcalf. 1985. "Exercise during pregnancy: Symposium on medical aspects of exercise." *Med. Clin. N. Amer.* 69:97–108.

Mullinax, K. M., and E. Dale. 1986. "Some considerations of exercise during pregnancy." *Clinics Sports Med.* 5:559–70.

National Dairy Council. 1980. "Nutrition and human performance." *Dairy Counc. Dig.* 51:13–17.

National Strength and Conditioning Association. 1989. "Strength training for female athletes: A position paper: Part I." *Nat. Strength Conditioning Assoc. J.* 11:43–56.

National Strength Coaches Association. 1986. "Periodization." *NSCA Journal* 8:12–22.

Olsson, K., and B. Saltin. 1971. "Diet and fluids in training and competition." *Scand. J. Rehabil. Med.* 3:31–38.

Page, L., and E. Phippard. 1957. "Essentials of an adequate diet." *Home Economics Research Report No. 3.* U.S. Department of Agriculture, Washington, D.C.

Pernow, B., and B. Saltin, eds. 1971. *Muscle Metabolism During Exercise.* New York: Plenum Press.

Puhl, J. L., and C. H. Brown. 1986. *The Menstrual Cycle and Physical Activity.* Champaign, Ill.: Human Kinetics Publishers.

Sale, D. G. 1988. "Neural adaptations to resistance training." *Med. Sci. Sports Exerc.* 20:S135–45.

Sanborn, C. F., B. J. Martin, and W. W. Wagner. 1982. "Is athletic amenorrhea specific to runners?" *Am. J. Obstet. Gynecol.* 143:859–66.

Shangold, M., and G. Mirkin. 1988. *Women and Exercise: Physiology and Sports Medicine.* Philadelphia: F. A. Davis Co.

Smith, N. 1981. "Nutrition and athletic performance." *Medical Times* 109:91–107.

Smith, N. J. 1976. *Food for Sport.* Palo Alto, Calif.: Bull Publishing Co.

Tesch, P. A. 1984. "Muscle capillary supply and fiber type characteristics in weight and power lifters." *J. Appl. Physiol.: Respirat. Environ. Exerc. Physiol.* 56:35–38.

Trujillo, C. 1983. "The effect of weight training and running exercise intervention on the self-esteem of college women." *Int. J. Sport. Psych.* 14:162–73.

Wells, C. L. 1985. *Women, Sport and Performance.* Champaign, Ill.: Human Kinetics Publishers.

Williams, M. H. 1976. *Nutritional Aspects of Human Physical and Athletic Performance.* Springfield, Ill.: Charles C. Thomas.

Williams, M. H., ed. 1983. *Ergogenic Aids in Sport.* Champaign, Ill.: Human Kinetics Publishers.

Wright, J. 1980. "Anabolic steroids and athletics." *Exerc. and Sports Sci. Rev.* 8:149–202.

Young, A., M. Stokes, J. M. Round, and R. H. T. Edwards. 1983. "The effect of high-resistance training on the strength and cross-sectional area of the human quadriceps." *Eur. J. Clin. Invest.* 13:411–17.

Young, D. R. 1977. *Physical Performance, Fitness, and Diet.* Springfield, Ill.: Thomas.

Index